D1246971

Volume **3**
of fifteen volumes

WORLD
AND
SPACE

CHILDCRAFT

The How and Why Library

FIELD ENTERPRISES EDUCATIONAL CORPORATION
CHICAGO
LONDON • ROME • STOCKHOLM • SYDNEY • TORONTO

Acknowledgments

The publishers of CHILDCRAFT, *The* How and Why
Library, gratefully acknowledge the courtesy of
the following publishers, agencies, and corporations for permission to use copyrighted illustrations. Full illustration acknowledgments for this
volume appear on pages 348–349.

California Institute of Technology: photography, pages
22–23, 98–99, copyright by California Institute of Technology.
Curtis Publishing Co.: photography by Bill Shrout, pages
196–197, courtesy *The Saturday Evening Post,* copyright
1961 by Curtis Publishing Co.
National Geographic Society: photography by Robert Goodman, Black Star, page 240, copyright by National Geographic Society.
Rand McNally & Co.: map, pages 216–217, copyright by
Rand McNally & Co.
Time, Inc.: photography, page 263, courtesy *Life* Magazine, copyright by Time, Inc.

CONTENTS

VOLUME 3 *World and Space*

Up in the Sky 4

Rain, Snow, and Sleet 34

Dew, Dust, and Fog 56

Winds and Breezes 74

A Trip Through Space 96

Deep Under the Ground 128

Rocks, Sand, and Soil 146

A Trip Across the Land 172

Where Am I? 208

A Trip at Sea 230

Tumbling, Flowing, and Flooding . . . 258

Fires and Explosions 282

Round, Square, and Bumpy 304

Again and Again 328

Illustration Acknowledgments 348

Volume Index 350

UP IN THE SKY

What does it take to make a sky?

First you take a lot of space,

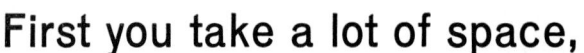

and fill some of it  with air.

Sprinkle in some stars,

then add one moon,

and top it off with a sun so bright
it covers up the stars.

Now scatter some clouds—

fluffy,

dark,

or wispy.

Flavor it with SPRINGTIME,

season it with SUMMER,

color it with AUTUMN,

or ice it with WINTER,

AND YOU HAVE A SKY!

What's in a Sunbeam?

A sunbeam makes a warm place for a cat to curl,
a shiny place for cobwebs to glisten,
or a spotlight for drifting bits of dust.
But a sunbeam is much more than these things.
It is part of sunlight.
And sunlight comes in many colors—
red,
orange,
yellow,
green,
blue,
indigo,
and violet.
All these different colored lights mix together
until there seems to be no color at all—
just light—
light to see the cat,
the cobweb,
the dust,
or anything else around you.

THE BIG BALL OF FIRE
IN THE SKY

The sun is our daytime star.
It is a huge ball of
spinning,
churning gases
that flare
and burst
into hundreds of atomic explosions
that spurt flames way out into space.
The sun is far away,
but it's not nearly as far away as the other stars
that twinkle at night.

The sun is hot enough and close enough
to warm up the world
and make it a place where we can live.

And the sun is bright enough and close enough
to light up the world,
and shine so brightly that all the other stars
that are farther away than our sun
seem to disappear in the daytime.

Why

IS THE SKY BLUE?

The sky usually looks blue—
not pink, red, green, or yellow!
It gets its blue color from the sunlight
that shines through the air.
Sunlight contains all the colors of the rainbow,
but these colors are scattered
as they pass through the air.
Some colors are scattered more than others,
and the color that is scattered the most
is the color you see—blue.

The sky usually looks light blue.
But if you went to the top of the highest mountain,
where there is less air between you and the sun
to scatter the sunlight,
the sky would be a deep, dark blue.
And if you rode in a rocket high above the earth,
where there is no air at all to scatter the sunlight,
the sky would be so dark that it would look black.

Sometimes the sky doesn't look blue.
At sunrise and sunset, the light from the sun
sometimes is scattered in such a way
that you see red, orange, and other colors in the sky.

THE SHAPES THAT

There's a tiger in the sky
looking down at me.
It seems about to roar,
but before it can
it turns into an elephant.
Or is it a giant cauliflower,
or a dragon in the middle of a yawn?
It is really a cloud for a sunny day
that changes shape as it floats through the air.

There's a fog up in the sky.
It is blotting out the sun
and making things look gloomy.

FLOAT IN THE SKY

It is really a cloud for a dark stormy day
that slides by in the sky,
and it often brings streaks of rain slashing to the ground.

There are feathers in the sky—
or are they the tails of invisible horses?
They are really the kind of clouds that float high up.
They hardly seem to move at all in a summer sky

The shapes of clouds often help people
know what the weather is going to be like.

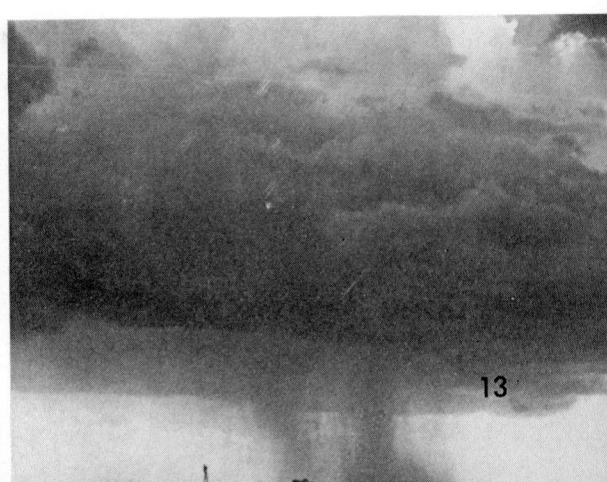

WHAT ARE CLOUDS MADE OF?

Clouds are really drops of water
floating in the sky.
These waterdrops are so small you can't see them,
but they cling together to make big clouds.
They make rain clouds,
snow clouds,
or fair-weather clouds.

14

WHERE DO CLOUDS GO?

Perhaps you have watched a big cloud
moving across the sky—
but when you looked for the cloud again,
it had disappeared.
Where did the cloud go?
It may have been blown away by the wind,
or it may have broken up into tiny clouds.
But it probably disappeared because its drops of water
fell to the earth as rain or snow.

15

WHAT MAKES A RAINBOW?

The sky is usually dark and cloudy when it rains.
And when the sun shines, the sky is bright and clear.
But sometimes
there is rain and sunshine in the sky at the same time.
Then,
like magic, beautiful bands of colors
arch across the gray sky.

A rainbow happens only
when sunshine and raindrops come together.
When sunlight shines through raindrops,
the light breaks up and scatters into many colors.
The sunlight scatters into
a band of red light,
a band of yellow light,
a band of green light,
a band of blue light,
and a band of violet light.

But sometimes, if the sun is shining,
you can make your own rainbow.
Turn the lawn sprinkler on.
Stand with your back to the sun
and look at the spray.

You will usually see a rainbow
made of sprinkler drops and sunshine.
You can also see rainbows
in the mist of a waterfall,
or in the spray of the sea,
or in water fountains.

Sometimes when mountain climbers
and airplane pilots
are way up high, they look down and see rainbows
that are whole circles of color.

RING
AROUND
THE MOON

When you see a ring around the moon,
it usually means that a storm is coming.
The ring is not really around the moon—
it only seems to be.
The ring is made when the moon shines
on high clouds
that are filled with tiny bits of ice.
The light from the moon shines on the bits of ice.
And as the light shines on the ice,
it bends and scatters to make a ring of light.
Sometimes two bright spots,
that look like little moons,
can be seen in the ring.
They are called "moon dogs."
During the day, we can sometimes see
a ring around the sun, and we can
also see "sun dogs."
A ring around the sun usually means
that a storm is coming, too.

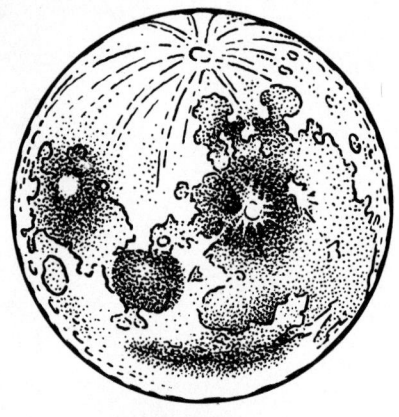

SHADOW PICTURES
ON THE MOON

What pictures do you see on the moon,
when it glows like a big button in the night sky?

Do you see a face—
the face of the man in the moon
looking down at you?

Do you see a picture of a donkey,
or a jumping rabbit?
Or do you see a man with a dog,
or a woman reading a book?

Whatever the picture you see,
it is a picture made by shadows—
sharp shadows of mountains and cliffs
that cover the moon.
The sun shines against the mountains and cliffs,
and sends shadows stretching across the moon.
The shadows mingle
and mix,
until,
if you look long enough
and hard enough,
you can see almost any picture
in the shadows of the moon.

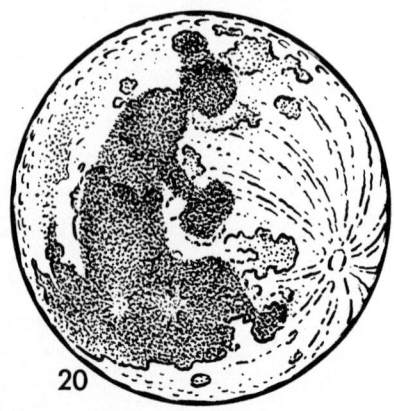

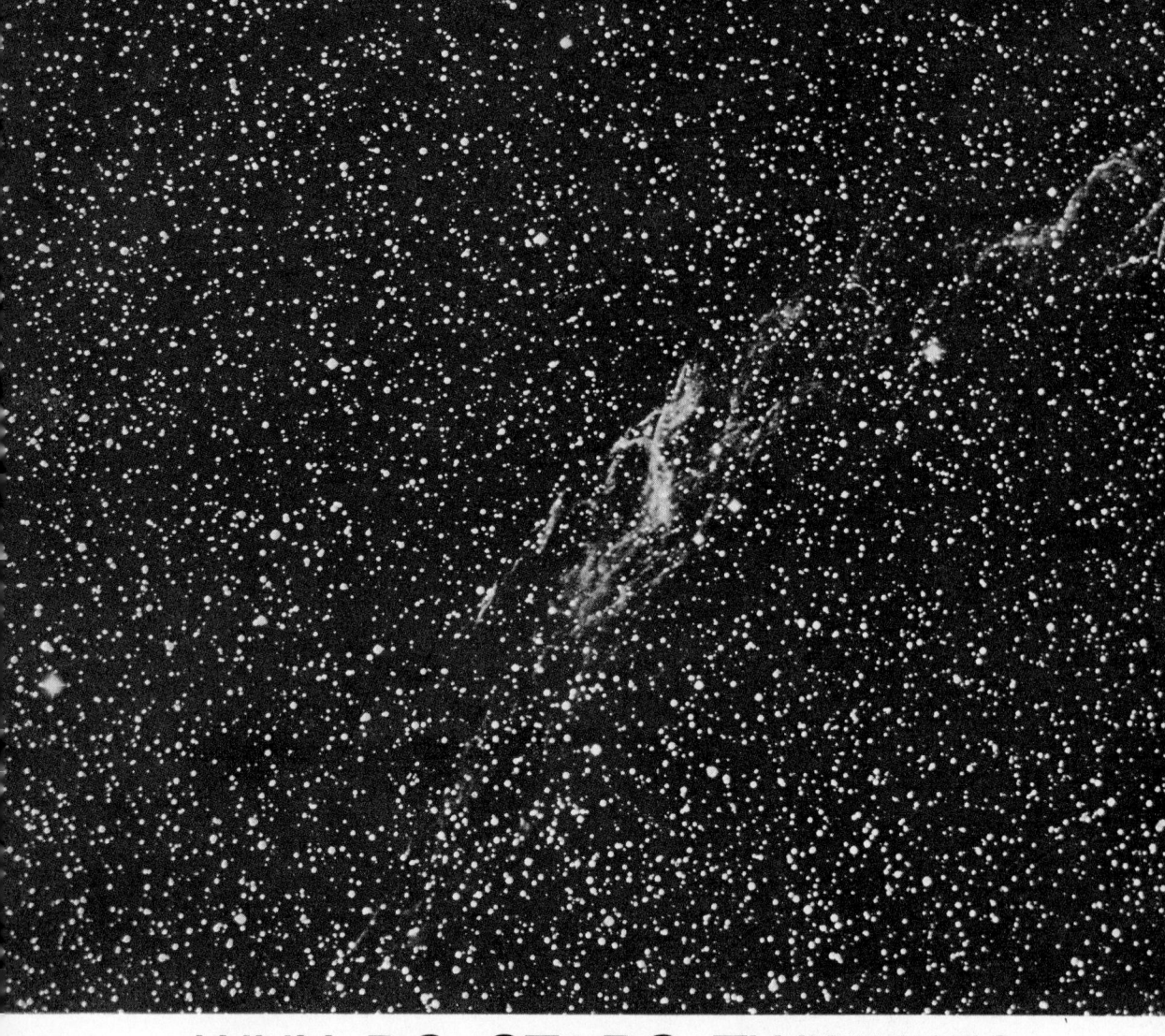

WHY DO STARS TWINKLE?

Twinkle, twinkle, little star—
why do stars twinkle?

Air makes stars twinkle.
As the light from a star shines down on earth,
it passes through the air around the earth.
The air is always moving and changing.
The changes are small,
but they make the starlight bend and scatter.
And this is why a star twinkles.

The astronauts who have
soared through space where there is no air
saw stars that didn't twinkle.

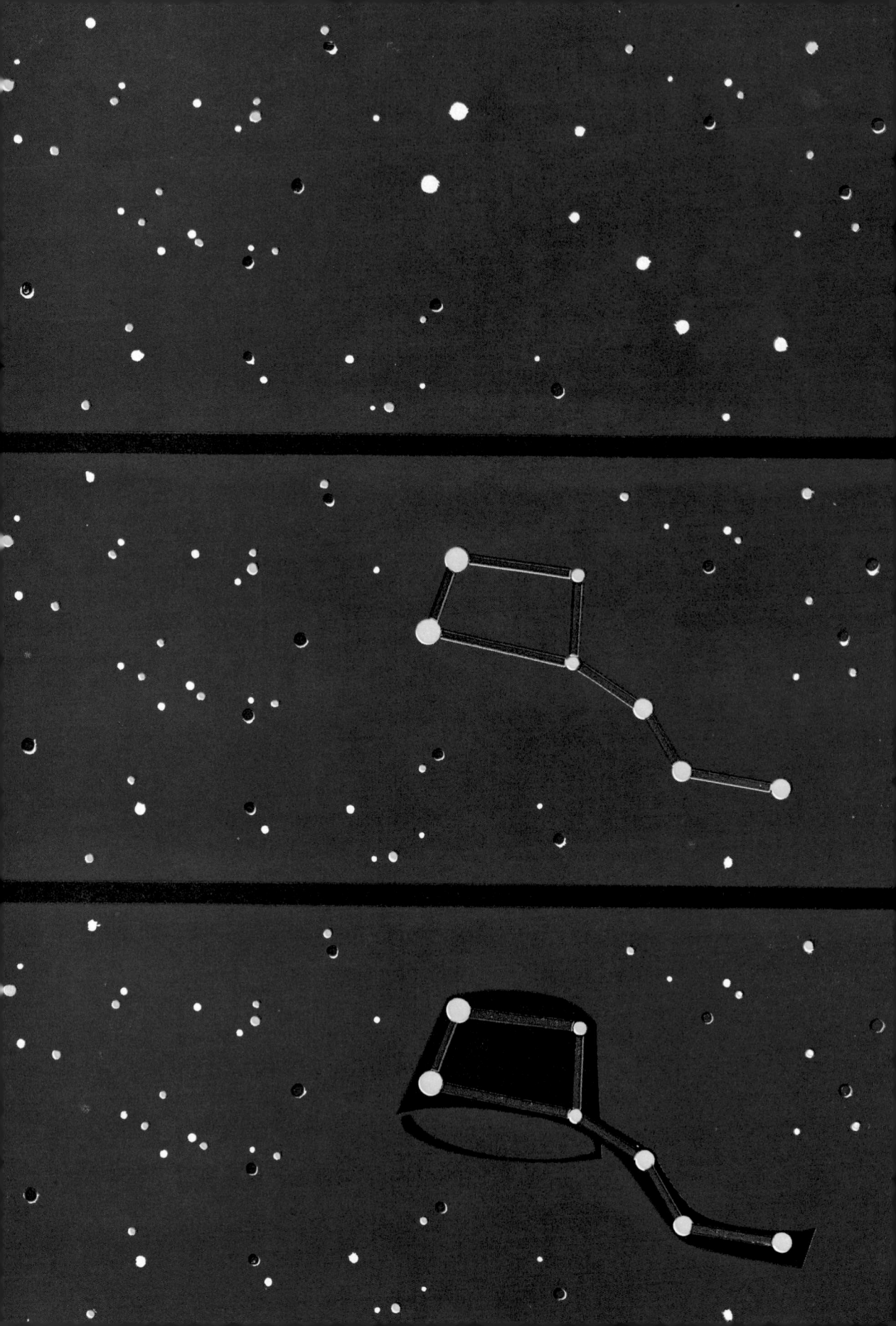

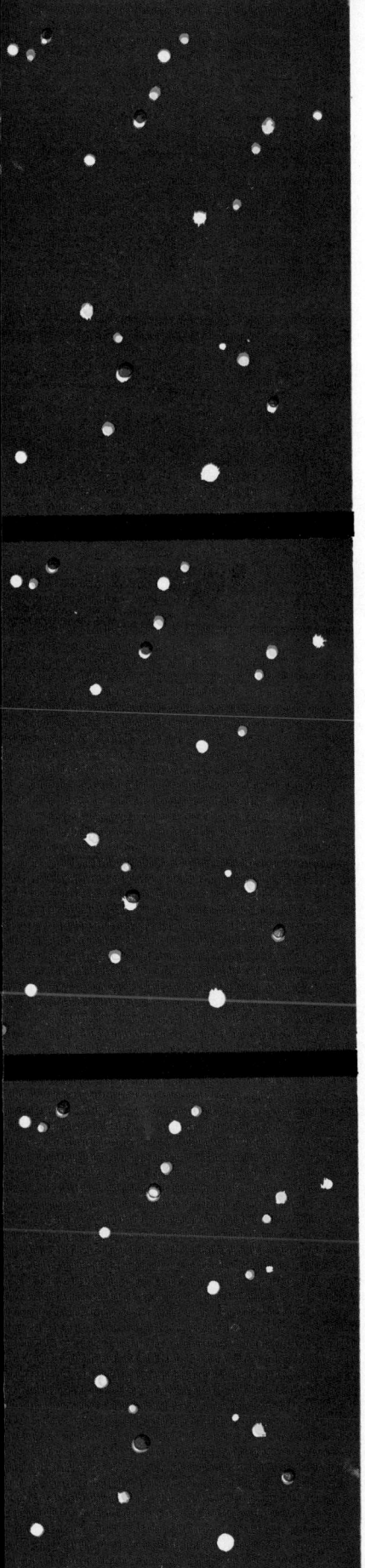

SKY-DOT PICTURES

The stars in the sky
seem to be all mixed together.
But if you look at them long enough,
you can make pictures out of them.
You can play a "follow-the-dot" game.
Imagine that you have a giant crayon
and that you can draw a line
from one star to another.
Then you can make sky-dot pictures!

Long, long ago, people began playing
the sky-dot game with stars.
They made pictures that looked like
people, animals, and things.
They made pictures of
the Big Dipper,
the Little Dipper,
the Big Bear,
the Little Bear,
Leo the Lion,
Pegasus, the horse with wings,
and Orion, the mighty hunter.

What kind of sky-dot pictures can you make?

SHOOTING STAR

STREAKS IN THE NIGHT

A METEOR STORM

Look up at the sky on a dark, clear night. If you look long enough, you will see a streak of light across the sky. The streak disappears almost as soon as you see it.

You may have to watch the sky for a long time before you see a streak of light.

At other times you may see several streaks of light, one after the other.

On some nights you may see a shower of them all at once.

We call the streaks of light "shooting stars" or "falling stars." But they really are not stars.

What are "falling stars"?

The streaks of light come from bits of rock and metal flying through space. There are millions and millions of these rock and metal pieces.

Some of them fall into the air that surrounds the earth. The bits of rock and metal speed through the air. They get hot and glow with a bright light.

If they are small, they burn up before they hit the ground. The streaks of light are the burning bits of rock and metal.

If they are large, they hit the ground and sometimes make big holes.

The bits of rock and metal are called meteors before they hit the ground. The ones that hit the earth are called meteorites.

ARIZONA METEOR CRATER

COLORED "CURTAINS" IN THE SKY

On some dark, clear nights,
there are streamers of colored lights high in the sky,
that look like curtains waving in the wind.
These are the northern lights
that shimmer and glow in the sky.
They start out as tiny flickers,
but grow and grow until
sometimes they cover the whole sky.
Sometimes they're pink,
and other times they're green.
But usually the lights are pure white.
They make big swatches of light
that zigzag up and down
and across the sky.

How did the "curtains" get up in the sky?
They came from the sun.
Along with the heat and light
that the sun sends out,
it also shoots out bits of electricity.
Most of the electricity is pulled
toward the North and South Poles of the earth.
When the electricity reaches the gases
that surround the earth,
the electricity makes
the gases glow in many colors.

If you live close to the North Pole, you're lucky.
The northern lights
are brighter and clearer there.
People who live near the South Pole
see colored lights, too.
These are called the southern lights.

When Your Ears Fill Up

Do you know why your ears sometimes seem to fill up
when you ride up in an elevator,
or when you go up in an airplane?
They do not really fill up.
You feel the air that is already inside your ears
pushing out.
But why does it push out
when you go up?

The answer is that air is always pushing against you.
And the air nearest the ground pushes against you
more than the air high in the sky pushes against you
when you go up in an airplane.
When you are on the ground,
the air outside your ear
pushes just as much as the air inside your ear,
and you never feel it.

But when you go up from the ground,
your ears are still filled with air from near the ground,
and this air pushes out just as much
as it did when you were on the ground.
Since the air outside your ear doesn't push
as much as the air inside your ear,
your ears seem to fill up.
When this happens, just yawn.

A yawn will let out the air you brought up with you—
sometimes with a pop!
And once your ears have cleared,
they fill up with the air around you.
Once again,
the air inside your ears pushes
just as much as the air outside.

A LITTLE BIT
OF SUNLIGHT

You are eating a little bit of sunlight
every time you eat food.
Sunlight carries energy.
Plants store energy from the sun,
and use it as they grow.
And when animals eat plants,
they store the energy from the sun
in their bodies.
When we eat plants and animals,
we eat the energy from the sun
that they stored up.

When you sit in front of a fire,
you could say that it's almost like sitting in the sun.
Because the glow you see
and the warmth you feel
is just energy from the sun
escaping from the coal.
Long ago,
plants that stored the energy, died.
And after millions of years,
the plants, and the energy they stored,
turned to coal.

RAIN, SNOW, AND SLEET

Henny-Penny was picking up corn
in the barnyard when—

WHACK!

Something hit her
on the head.

"Mercy me!" squawked Henny-Penny,
"The sky is falling!"
She ran down the road to tell her friends,

Cocky-Locky,

Ducky-Daddles,

Goosey-Poosey,

and Turkey-Lurkey.

What *did* fall from the sky
and hit Henny-Penny?

34

If she had looked,
instead of running,
she might have seen a big,

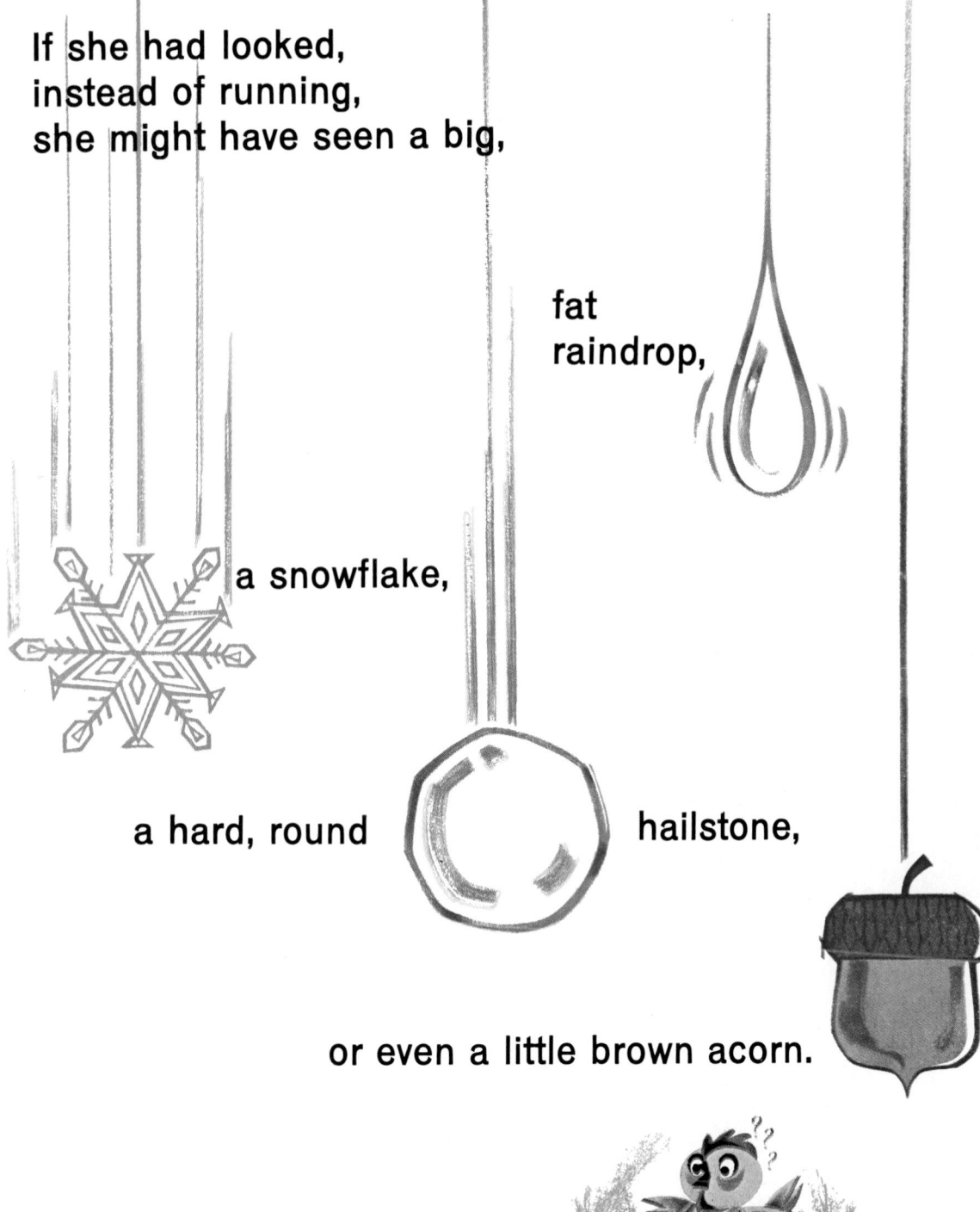

fat
raindrop,

a snowflake,

a hard, round   hailstone,

or even a little brown acorn.

Poor, silly Henny-Penny!
On the next few pages
you will read about rain, snow, sleet,
and other things that fall from the sky.

WHERE DOES RAIN COME FROM?

Did you know that water to make raindrops
comes from beneath your feet?—
from lakes, rivers, oceans, plants,
and even animals?
Water has to go up
before it can come down.
When water goes up into the air,
we say that it has "evaporated."
And when this same water comes down again,
we say that it has "rained."

You can't see water evaporate,
but you know that it does
because, when the sun shines,
puddles disappear,
clothes dry on the line,
water in lakes, rivers,
and even in fishbowls, gets lower,
plants sag and wilt,
dogs pant,
and little boys drink lots of water.

When enough water has gone up into the air,
it falls again as raindrops.
The water in the raindrops makes
the same trip over and over again—
down to the ground,
then back up into the air.

Drizzles, Downpours, and Sprinkles

When water falls from the sky,
it may drizzle,
or sprinkle,
or just pour.

A drizzle may not look
like rain at all.
It's a slow-falling fuzzy kind of fog
that drearily drifts down
with hardly a sound
and makes a gray day even grayer.

A sprinkle is thicker than a drizzle.
A sprinkle twinkles with fun
and falls with a patter.
It teases you outside
for a few romping games
then dances away to some
other place.

Just plain rain kicks up dust
when it first comes.
Then it beats the dust down
into the ground
and covers the yard with water.
It splashes across the windowpane
and leaves some dancing drops
for you to watch
while it drums on the roof
of the house.

A downpour is thicker
than just plain rain.
It smothers the window
with an angry sheet of water,
and it hammers at the house
with a roar.

39

YELLOW, RED, AND POLKA-DOT SNOW

Where can you build a yellow snowman?
Where can you throw brown snowballs?
Where can you walk in the snow,
and leave pink, red, blue, green,
or even polka-dot footprints?

Yellow snow often falls in very dusty places.
Bits of yellow dust in the air
stick to falling snowflakes
and make them look yellow.
In other dusty places,
if you built a snowman,
he might not be yellow,
but brown, or even red—
the color of the dust in the air.

Sometimes yellow snow falls over high mountains,
especially if the mountains
are covered with pine trees.
The snowflakes get their yellow color
from pine tree pollen floating in the air.

Red, pink, green, or blue snow
sometimes covers the ground in very cold places.
The snow is not really these colors—
the bright color comes
from tiny plants underneath it.
If the snow is very deep,
you might not see any color at all—
until you walk through the snow.
Then you'd be surprised to see
that you leave red, pink, green, or blue footprints.
And if the plants under the snow grow in patches,
you might even leave polka-dot footprints!

DRY-ICE CRYSTALS ARE DROPPED FROM AN AIRPLANE INTO CLOUDS.

How
To Make
Rain

You can't make rain by dancing.
Some American Indians tried it, and it didn't work.
But people *can* make rain in other ways.

To do it,
a weather pilot flies his airplane over big clouds.
Then he sprinkles the clouds with powder.
The powder is made of special chemicals.
It might be "dry ice,"
or it might be silver iodide.
"Dry ice" freezes tiny drops of water
in the clouds into ice lumps
so heavy that they fall.
As the ice lumps fall through the warm air,
they melt into big drops of rain.
Silver iodide causes many tiny drops
of water to stick to it.
Soon there is enough water
around each bit of silver iodide
to make a raindrop.
And when the raindrop is heavy enough,
it falls to the ground.

But even weather pilots can't always make it rain.
If the clouds aren't big and full of water,
and if there isn't a lot of moisture in the air,
cloud sprinkling won't work.

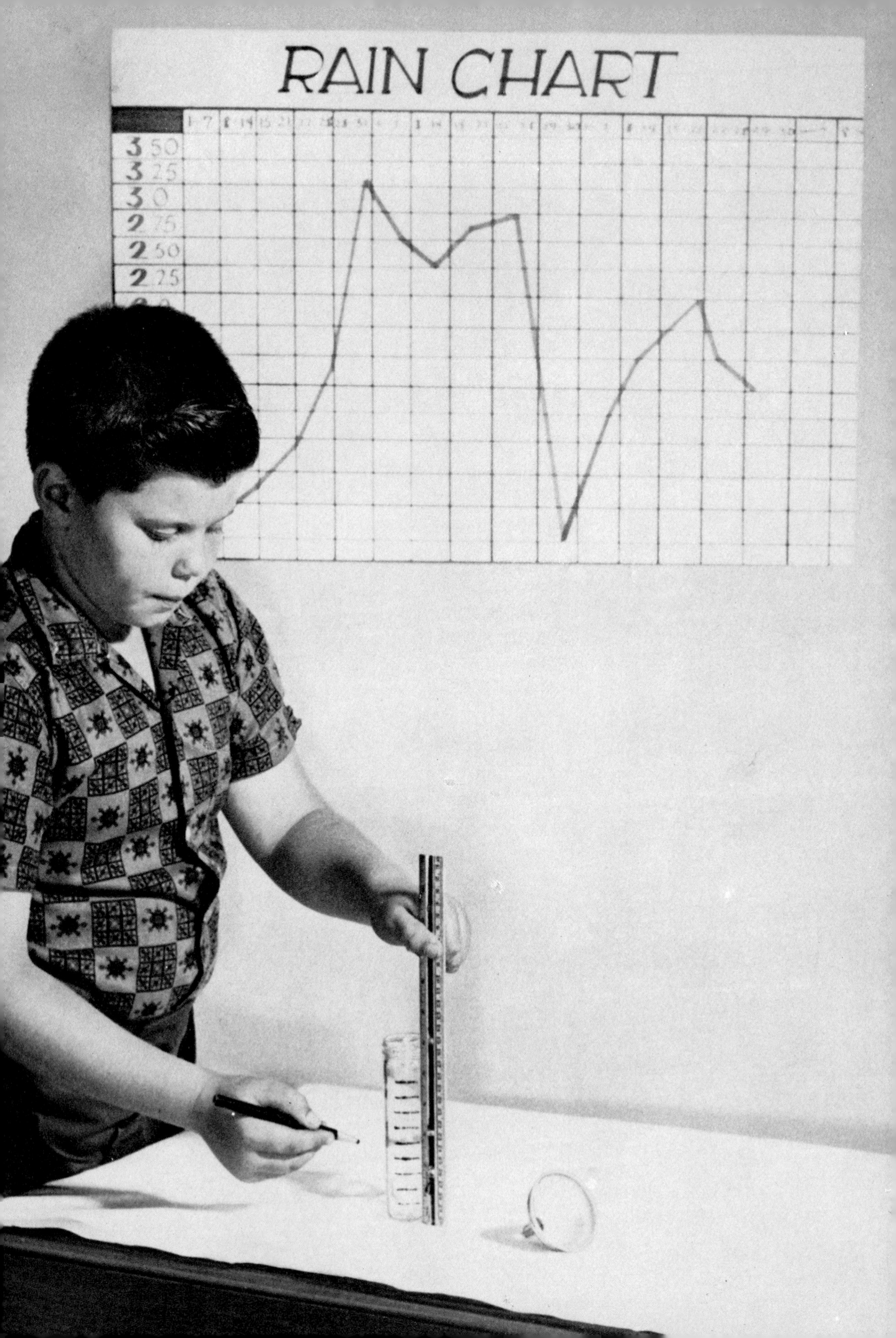
RAIN CHART
3 50
3 25
3 0
2 75
2 50
2 25

You Can Measure Rainfall

You can find out *how long* it rains
by watching a clock.
But it's a little harder to find out *how much* it rains.
You have to make a rain gauge.

You will need a straight-sided bottle,
such as an olive bottle,
a funnel, a ruler, and a black crayon.
Hold the ruler next to the bottle,
and mark off equal spaces on the side of the bottle.
Set the funnel inside the bottle,
and place the rain gauge outdoors
away from trees and bushes.

After a rain,
you can look at the markings on the bottle
to find out exactly how much rain fell.
Then empty the bottle
so it will be ready for the next rain.
Check the bottle after each rain.
Did it rain more or less today
than it rained the last time?

You may want to keep a record or chart
to see how much rain falls
during a day, a week, or a month.

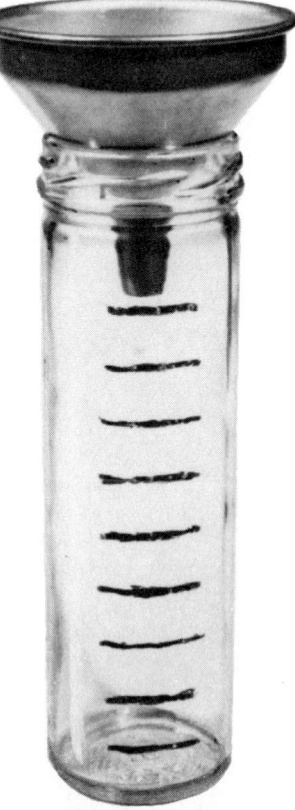

HAIL OR SLEET

Some people think the only difference between hail and sleet
is that hailstones are usually larger than sleet.
But hailstones can be as small as the head of a pin
or as large as an orange.
The real difference between hail and sleet
is in how they're made.

Hailstones begin as tiny frozen raindrops
high up in storm clouds.
As these tiny hailstones fall through the clouds,
they pick up drops of water.
But before they can fall to the ground,
strong winds toss them high in the air again.
Then water freezes around the hailstones—layer upon layer—
until they're heavy enough to fall.
Sometimes the wind bounces them up and down in the clouds
for a long time before they fall.

Sleet starts as very cold drops of water
that fall through the air from clouds.
As these waterdrops fall through cold air on their way down,
they freeze together into beads of ice that we call sleet.

An easy way to find out if a lump of ice is hail or sleet
is to split it in two.
If the lump of ice is made of layers—
like those inside an onion—it is hail.
But if the lump is solid ice, it is probably sleet.

WHAT ARE SNOWFLAKES?

In wintertime,
when it is cold enough to prickle your nose,
snowflakes often fall.
Snow comes from clouds
that are damp and heavy
with thousands of tiny waterdrops.
Each tiny waterdrop freezes around
a bit of ash, or sand, or dust,
in the frigid air.

And as each waterdrop freezes,
it grows and becomes a tiny ice crystal.
A crystal has a special shape—
usually a flat, smooth surface
that has sharp edges and corners.
Things that can become crystals
always turn into crystals
with a certain number of corners.

Salt always turns into a crystal
with eight corners.
Borax always turns into a crystal
with twelve corners.
Water always turns into a crystal
with six corners.
Because a snowflake is a crystal of water,
it always has six corners.

Six-cornered snowflakes are tossed
and twirled by the wind
until they pile up, end to end,
side by side, one on top of another,
to make a snowdrift, a cap on a fencepost,
or an outline on every twig of a tree. **49**

dry and wet snow

It's fun to have
a snowball fight
or to make a snowman.
But sometimes a snowball
crumbles in your hands
when you try to round it out.

50

Why does some snow pack
into snowballs,
while other snow does not?

If it is very cold outside,
the snow that falls
on the ground stays mostly dry.
And dry snow does not pack.

But if it is not so cold outside,
or if the ground is warm,
the snow that falls on the ground
may melt a little,
and then the snow is wet.
And wet snow packs
so that you can make
snowballs
and snowmen!

WHAT WILL THE WEATHER BE?

There are many old rhymes that tell you what the weather will be. Some are just silly, but some —like these—are true.

Rainbow at night
is the sailors' delight;
Rainbow at morning,
sailors take warning.

Mackerel sky,
Soon wet or dry.

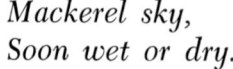

When the dew is on the grass,
Rain will never come to pass.

Rainbows form when sunlight shines through raindrops. The sun moves from east to west, and rain usually moves from west to east. So an evening rainbow appears in the east, which means that the rain has passed. But a morning rainbow comes in the west, which means that rain will soon begin.

Mackerel clouds are clouds that look like the scales on fish. They can grow into rainclouds, or they may be pieces of clouds left over from the last rain.

At night, plants lose heat and get cold. This causes water in the air to condense and stick to the plants as dew. If rainclouds are overhead, like a blanket, heat from the plants won't go up, and dew does not form.

CAN ANIMALS FORECAST

People used to think that animals knew
when the weather was going to be bad.

Even today, some people think . . .

The more nuts squirrels gather in
the fall, the colder the coming
winter will be.

If the stripes around woolly bear
caterpillars are wide, the coming
winter will be mild. But if their
stripes are narrow, a cold winter is
ahead.

If a ground hog sees its shadow on
February 2, cold weather will last
six more weeks. If the ground hog
doesn't see his shadow, spring will
be early.

Flies bite more before a storm.

Frogs croak more and ducks quack
louder before a rain.

When birds migrate to another home, they fly only
over places where there will be no storms.

THE WEATHER?

But we know that . . .

Squirrels gather all the nuts they can find.

Some woolly bear caterpillars' stripes are wide, and some are narrow. This has nothing to do with the weather.

Whether or not one day is sunny cannot mean that a winter will be long or short.

Flies bite just as much before fair weather as they do before a storm.

Frogs croak and ducks quack to get the attention of other frogs and ducks.

Many migrating birds are killed because they fly into heavy storms.

55

DEW, DUST, AND FOG

Where does dust drift?
IN THE AIR.

Where does fog roll?
IN THE AIR.

Where does frost gleam?
IN THE AIR.

Where does smoke billow?
IN THE AIR.

On the next few pages,

you will find out how, without air,

there would be no fog to hide things from you,

no frost to paint windowpane pictures,

no smoke to get in your eyes,

no dew to glisten on a cobweb,

and no dust to swirl about you.

THE OCEAN YOU CAN'T SEE

You walk,
run,
play,
eat, and sleep on the bottom of an ocean.
The ocean is really
an invisible ocean of air
that covers the world like the skin of an orange.

What is air? Air is different kinds of gases.
Air is also
tiny drops of water too small to see
and bits of dust and dirt.

The gases, the water, and the dirt are
mingled and mixed together
to make the
air you breathe,
the air that blows in your face as a breeze,
the air that smells like dinner cooking,
and the air that can carry the sound
of your voice when you speak.

FOG AND SMOG

What sort of day can it be,
when you hear the footsteps
of an invisible man
and the bark of an invisible dog?
What kind of a day is it,
when you can feel an itch
at the end of your nose,
but can't see the finger you use to scratch it?

It is a foggy day—
a day when the cold ground
chills a warm, damp breeze
and turns the dampness
into tiny droplets of water.
As the many tiny droplets
come together, they form
wisps of cloud.
And as more and more dampness turns
to more and more water droplets,
the wisps of cloud get thicker and thicker
until they cover the ground.
And that's what a fog really is—
just a cloud on the ground.

WHAT IS SMOG?

Take the SM from the word SMOKE,
and the OG from the word FOG.
Put them together, and you have SMOG.
And that's what SMOG really is—
just mixed-up smoke and fog.

61

WHAT IS DUST?

62

Dust is more than just bits of grit
and tiny specks of dirt.
Dust can be bits of bats' wings,
butterflies' tongues,
flies' wings,
and dried-up pieces of caterpillar skin.

Dust can be tiny chips worn off a rock by rain and wind,
a bit of a whisker left by a mouse,
or a speck of soot from a faraway chimney.

Dust can be
dandelion fluff,
or powdered rose petals.
It can be ground-up bird feathers,
or nutshell crumbs dropped by a squirrel.

If you look at dust through a microscope,
you will see that dust is a mixture of all these things
and many more.
Dust drifts in the air until a breeze
sprinkles it on a window sill,
or swirls it into balls of fluff under the bed.

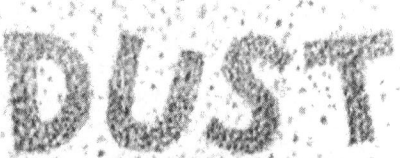

DUST from Outer Space

Part of the dust you walk on comes from outer space. It is called cosmic dust.

Bits of rock and metal are always floating around in space. Some of them speed toward the earth. When they hit the air that surrounds the earth, they burn up. When we see them burn, we call them "shooting stars."

Then the ashes and cinders from the shooting stars slowly drift down from the sky.

Cosmic dust looks so much like earth dust that it falls to the ground without anyone noticing it.

But there really is cosmic dust beneath our feet. If you would like to see some, the next page tells you how to find it.

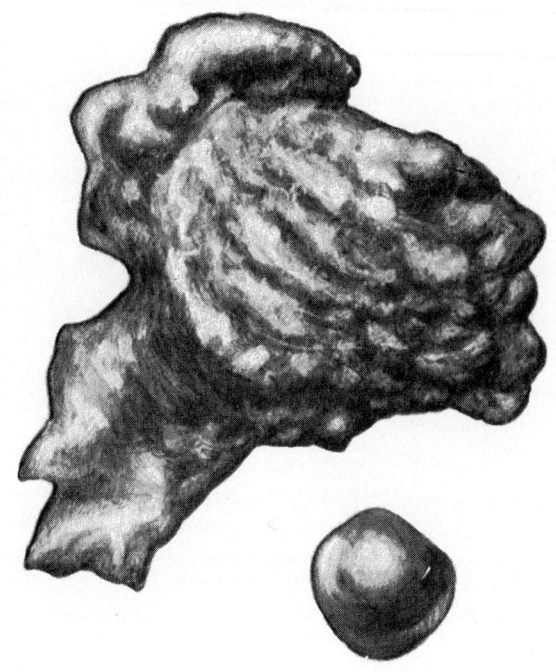

How To Find Dust from Outer Space

A magnet will pick up some cosmic dust. It will not pick up other dust.

Magnets will pick up bits of iron, as you know. And a magnet will pick up bits of cosmic dust made of iron.

If you look at this cosmic dust through a microscope, you can see that each bit of it is made of a tiny blob of metal.

Some bits look like round droplets, while others look like jagged cinders.

Cosmic dust looks different from earth dust.

Where Does Dew Come From?

Early in the morning,
dewdrops sparkle like jewels on a leaf.
They glisten on a spiderweb
and glitter on blades of grass.

But last night the dewdrops weren't there.
Last night the leaves were dry,
the grass was dry,
and the spiderweb was dry.

What makes the dew?

Dew is formed only when the air is damp
and when the air is warmer than the ground.

Then the dampness of the air sticks on the leaves,
the grass, and the spiderweb.
The tiny bits of water join each other
and grow into little drops.
The little drops join and grow into big drops.

Then you see dewdrops sparkling on the leaves,
glistening on a spiderweb,
and glittering on the grass.

Make Your Own Dewdrops

You can make dew.
You can make it with your breath
because your breath is warm and damp
like the morning air.
A windowpane is cold.
Blow gently on the windowpane.
Blow some more.
Little drops will come.
Blow some more.
Big drops will come.
Now you have made dew!

WINDOWPANE PICTURES

Early in the morning,
after a cold and starry night,
you may see icy pictures on your windowpane—
lacy pictures made of frost.

Frost forms when the air is damp
and the ground is freezing cold.
The cold chills each tiny drop of water
in the damp air.

The waterdrops get colder
and colder
until,
one by one,
they suddenly freeze into sparkling crystals of ice
that spread in feathery sprays
or swirl in lacy coils
across your windowpane.

THE PART

THAT NEVER BURNS

A log in a fire
sizzles
and hisses,
crackles, pops, and burns
until there is nothing left of the log
but a pile of embers glowing
on a bed of burned-out ashes.

But not all the log burns.
Thousands of tiny black bits of charred wood,
murky drops of water too small to see,
and all sorts of gases
curl
and drift into the air.
All these are what we call smoke.

Smoke is the part of the log that never burns,
but it can get in your throat and make you cough.
It can also get in your eyes and make you cry.

Saint Elmo's Fire

In stormy weather,
when thunder rumbles
and lightning streaks the sky,
a sailor may suddenly see
ghostly flames
flickering
and dancing
on the masts of his ship at sea.

The sailor won't be frightened
because he will know
that it is Saint Elmo's Fire.
He knows it is really a fire of electricity
that won't burn and won't hurt anyone.
During a storm, some of the electricity
in the air moves into the ship.
More and more electricity piles up
in the plunging ship.
Because there is so much electricity
in the ship, it cannot hold any more.
Then, with a sudden glow of eerie light,
the stored-up electricity
shoots back into the air
out the top of the masts.

Sometimes you can see
Saint Elmo's Fire on the land, too.
Sometimes it dances from
chimney tops,
or tall church steeples.
It can even flicker along a horse's mane,
or glow around a person's head
without hurting him.

WINDS AND BREEZES

What can you feel but cannot see?
What can hurl a car into a tree?

What can make a flag flutter
or a leaf tumble?
What can blow dust into whirling clouds?

What can whistle and howl?

What can pull trees up from their roots?
What can pull houses into the sea?

Wind can do all these things,
and many more.
READ ON AND SEE.

WHERE DOES
WIND COME FROM?

You have a wind in your kitchen every day.
You may not feel it,
but it is there.

If the kitchen stove is turned on,
all the air above the stove is heated.
When air gets hot, it swells and becomes lighter.
Then cooler, heavier air
pushes up the warmer, lighter air,
and takes its place.
This movement of the hot air going up,
and the cool air coming in
makes a wind.

The ground you walk on
is at the bottom of an ocean of air.
The air near the ground often swells,
and becomes hotter and lighter.
Then the cooler, heavier air pushes it up,
and takes its place.
This movement of air makes
a wind
or a breeze.

What is Wind?

Wind can be many things.
It can be
a gentle breeze that
brushes your cheek,
rustles leaves,
and drifts smoke.

It can be
a strong breeze that
stings your face,
sways small trees,
and picks up dust and paper.

It can be
a gale that
rips at your clothes,
breaks tree twigs,
and whistles and bellows.

It can be
a strong gale that
pulls trees up from their roots,
blows roofs off houses,
and breaks windows.

CAN IT?

Can a sail billow in a **bull's eye**
or a flag flutter in a **cat's paw**?

Can a **chinook** ruffle your hair
or a **sirocco** get sand in your eyes?

Can you smell dinner in a **wisper,**
or feel a **whirly** on your cheek?

Can a **harmattan**
pick up leaves,
and can smoke drift
in a **zephyr?**

Can you feel a **williwaw** in a mountain,
and can a **simoom** make you sneeze?

Can a **bad-i-sad-o-bistroz**
whistle,
and is **Santa Ana** dusty?

The answer to all these
questions is YES,
because they are all names
of different kinds of WINDS.

WHIRLING MOUNTAINS

There are huge mountains of air
whirling around us.
You cannot see them
because you cannot see air.
But if you could see them,
they would look like
mountains
with peaks high in the sky.

The weatherman calls
these mountains of air
high-pressure areas.
They bring
bright, sunny skies
and fair weather.

OF AIR

But sometimes there are whirling valleys of air
instead of mountains of air.
The weatherman calls these valleys of air
low-pressure areas.
In the low-pressure areas,
hot and wet air
and cold and dry air
from the high-pressure areas
mix to bring
gray, gloomy skies
and rain or snow.

The whirling mountains
and valleys of air
make the wind blow.
If the mountain
or the valley of air is small,
the wind hardly blows at all.
But as the mountain or the valley of air
gets bigger,
the wind blows harder and harder.

dust devils

A dust devil is something like a tornado.
A tornado starts in the sky
and whirls down to earth.
But a dust devil starts
on the ground
and whirls up.

In a desert,
you can see many dust devils
whirling at the same time.

When dust devils get big,
they are called pillars of sand.
They last for hours
and are sometimes as high as mountains.

You can see tiny dust devils
on any city street or country road
whenever it is hot and wind whirls
paper and dust upward.

A GIANT VACUUM CLEANER

A tornado is
a whirling, rushing wind
that roars over the ground
like a giant vacuum cleaner.
It pulls up dust and dirt,
explodes houses apart,
and hurls cars into the air.

A tornado starts
when a thick layer of cold air
flows over a thick layer of warm air.
Some of the cold air
pushes down into the layer of warm air
and some of the warm air rises
into the layer of cold air.
As the warm air rises, other warm air rushes in
to take its place.
This makes the air start to spin.
The more it rushes, the faster it spins,
until it *is* a heavy, black cloud
of whirling, rushing air and dust.

A tornado over the ocean is called a waterspout.
It is a funnel of water
instead of a funnel of air.

The Storm with an Eye

The air is muggy
and you can hardly breathe.
The sky is green, the wind is
blowing softly, and it is
starting to drizzle.
Then the wind blows harder
and harder,
and still harder.
The rain beats and pounds
on the roofs and sidewalks.

The wind blows roofs off houses,
knocks down trees,
breaks windows,
pulls houses into the sea,
and pushes ships onto the land.
It has such power and fury
that you know it is a hurricane!

A hurricane is like a giant whirlpool
with a hole in the middle called the eye.
When the eye of the hurricane
passes over your head,
the wind stops,
the rain stops,
and the sky is clear.

But in a little while,
the wind starts to whistle and bellow again
in another direction.
As the rain beats and pounds again,
everything is blown,
twisted, and tossed again.
It is the other half
of the swirling,
whirling hurricane
lashing out its fury.

89

HURRICANE HUNTERS

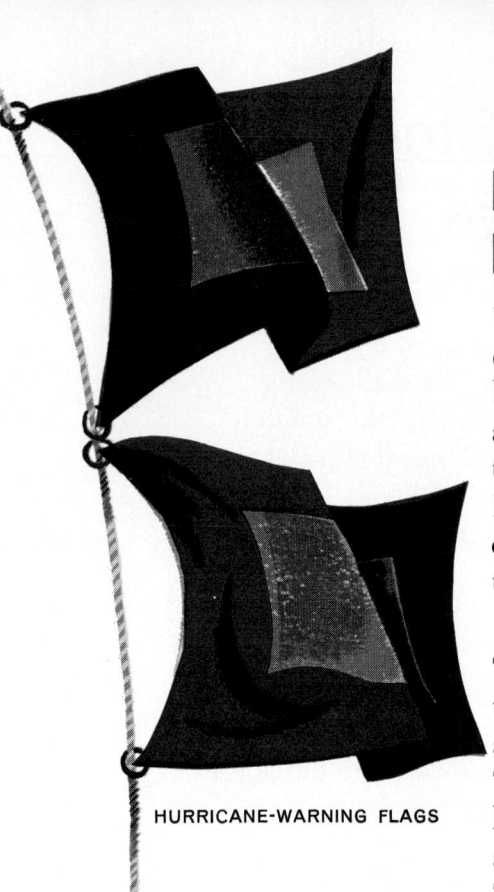

HURRICANE-WARNING FLAGS

When the power and fury
of a hurricane
bashes and crashes
against the shore,
there is nothing anyone can do to stop it.
But people who are hurricane hunters
can warn others
that a hurricane is coming.

There are hurricane hunters on land
that look at the sea waves
and the clouds.
They measure air pressure,
how warm the air is,
and how much water is in it.
Then they can tell if a hurricane is coming.

Sailors on ships are hurricane hunters
because all hurricanes begin over the ocean.

And some airplane pilots
are hurricane hunters.
They fly into the eye of the hurricane
and measure
how big the storm is
and how much force it has.

BLIZZARDS

When the weather is cold,
and the wind whistles and blows,
and soft, powdery snow falls
so thick
that you can hardly see,
we call it a blizzard.

Blizzards can
pile up big snowdrifts as high as your house
so that you cannot see out of your windows.
Snowdrifts can stall cars
and block roads,
and sometimes snarl up
big-city traffic for days.

MONSOONS

Some places that are near the sea
have windstorms, called monsoons,
during the summer.
The weather gets hot,
and strong winds blow
from the sea toward the land,
bringing rain that pelts and pounds
the ground.

Sometimes the wind blows and blows,
and the rain pounds and pounds,
day after day,
for almost as long as your summer vacation.

CLOUDS OF DUST

Did you ever see it rain mud?
When rain falls during a dust storm,
it comes down as mud.

The wind churns and blows
dust and dirt
from the ground
into the air
until you see nothing
but a whirling,
swirling cloud of dust.

It is no use to dust
during a dust storm.
No matter how much you dust,
there is always more dust to dust.

Sandstorms are the same as dust storms.
But the wind whirls and blows
clouds of sand
instead of clouds of dust.

A TRIP

Whoosh! Up, up above the clouds I zoom!
I am an astronaut going out into space.
As I look back,
I can see the earth looking like a great big ball.
And as the hours go by,
it gets smaller and smaller.

Now I'm racing past the Moon,
and the sun is so bright
it makes my eyes water.
A day has gone by—maybe two.

THROUGH SPACE

Suddenly, looming up ahead,
I see another world.
But before I can see
if it is like my world,
a mountain of rock
rushes past my rocket ship,
and I duck my head.

When I look out again,
the world I saw is far behind.
I wonder if there was someone
on that world
to see my rocket ship roaring past.
Now I'm on my way to other stars.
I wonder, how far I can go?

97

HOW MANY STARS ARE THERE?

How many stars are out tonight?
More than there are
snowflakes in a snowstorm,
or pebbles on a beach,
or freckles on a freckled face,
or leaves on a tree,
or grains of sand in a desert.

On a clear night you can see stars all over the sky.
And if you could look through a telescope,
you would see many, many more.
You would see more stars than there are
people in the world,
or raindrops in a rainstorm,
or fish in the ocean,
or birds in the sky,
or blades of grass in a meadow.

More stars are out at night
than have ever been counted.

UNUSUAL STARS

"Twinkle, twinkle, little star,
How I wonder what you are!
Up above the world so high,
Like a diamond in the sky."
Are you really white?
Or are you red, blue, green, or gold?
Maybe you're a yellow star bigger than the sun,
or a blazing white star that never stops exploding.

I wonder how big you are.
Are you a supergiant star
or just an ordinary giant star?
Are you one of those dwarf stars
so heavy that a tiny piece of you
could sink right into the earth?

I wonder if you are just one star,
or if that is your twin I see peeking from behind you?
Perhaps you are really three stars
spinning in a bunch?
Whatever kind of star you are,
you must be one of these.
But you are just too far away for me to know
what kind of star you really are.

THE TAIL OF A COMET

Some stars seem to have tails,
but, if they do, they are not really stars.
They are balls of rocks and gas, called comets,
that streak past the earth
with trails of stardust behind them.

Sunlight glitters on the stardust
making it gleam in the night sky.
Comets come from way out in space.
They rush past the earth,
sweep around the sun,
then whizz far out into space again.
The only time you can see a comet,
is when it passes close to the earth.

Halley's comet
is one that is big and bright.
It passes close to the earth about every 75 years—
just once in a lifetime.

Sounds in the Night

The creak of a cricket,
and the croak of a frog,
and the rustle of leaves in a breeze
are sounds you can hear on a starry night
when a whisper becomes as loud as a shout.

Stars make sounds, too.
They beep,
buzz,
whistle,
hum,
crackle,
ping,
and pop.

You can hear star sounds only
with a special machine,
called a radio telescope.
If you could use one,
you would hear the stars
just as easily as you hear
a cricket,
a frog,
a whisper,
or leaves in a breeze.

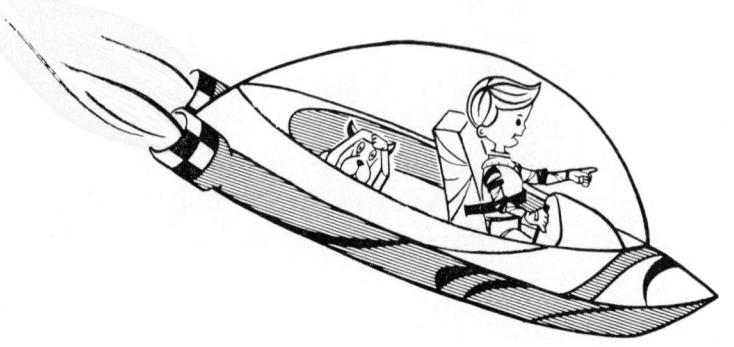

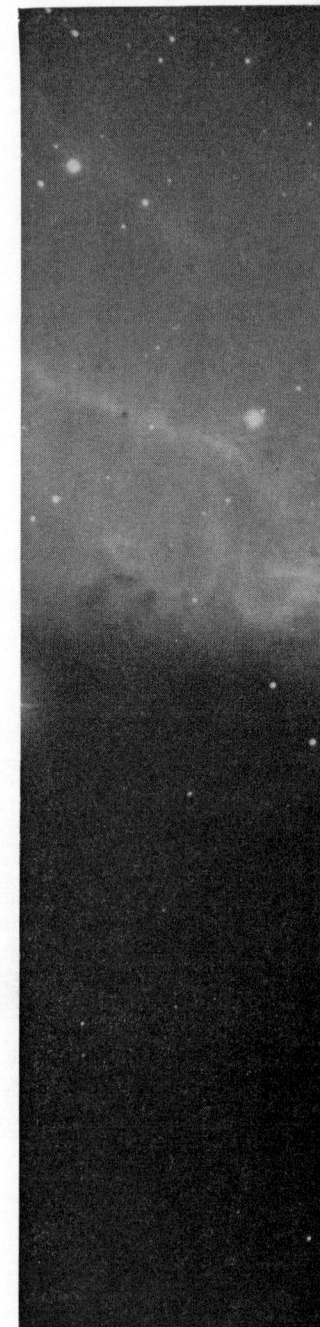

SPACE CLOUDS

If you were an astronaut
zooming through space—
way beyond the sky,
and past the Moon and Sun,
you would still see clouds—
but these clouds are made of rocks, gas,
and bits of dust.
Starlight glints against the dust,
shines off the rocks,
gleams through the gas,
and makes the clouds glow with silvery light.

But sometimes,
the dust is so thick,
and the gas is so dense,
that the cloud blots out the stars.
Then you can't see the stars behind the clouds,
and it looks as though
there is just a big black hole in the sky.

The horsehead nebula in Orion is a dark cloud
of gas and rock that looks something like a horse's head.

What Sort of Place?

Where would you be
if you could jump over a house,
talk without making a sound,
become invisible by stepping into a shadow,
or throw a ball so high
you would have to sit a while and wait for it to come down?

What sort of place is it
where the sky is always black,
even though the sun is shining,
where there is never a cloud in the sky,
never a cooling breeze—in fact no wind at all?

What sort of place could it be
when it would take a whole month
to get from one day to the next,
and where there are only twelve days
and twelve nights in a year?
There is such a place!
It is the Moon!

WHEN THINGS DON'T DROP

No matter how hard you try,
you can't drop anything
when you are speeding through outer space.
A glass won't smash
and a dish won't shatter
if an astronaut lets them
slip through his fingers.

Even if a cookie crumbles
as an astronaut eats it,
the crumbs won't drop.

Gravity is what makes things drop.
But in a rocket ship
that is far from the pull of gravity
and going very fast,
there's not enough gravity to pull the glass,
or the dish,
or the crumbs to make them drop.
So they just hang in the air,
as though held there by invisible threads.

WORLDS AROUND

The Earth is not the only world
that whirls around the sun.
There are other worlds called planets.
No one has ever been to them,
but people know a few things about them
because they have watched them
through telescopes.
We know Mercury is a world
that whirls around the sun.
Of all the worlds,
it is the hottest and the closest to the sun.

We know Venus is a world
that whirls around the sun.
It may be covered
with a boiling sea of gases,
or a sizzling desert
where winds blow all the time.

We know Mars is a world
that whirls around the sun.
It is a dying world of red and orange deserts
where people might have lived.

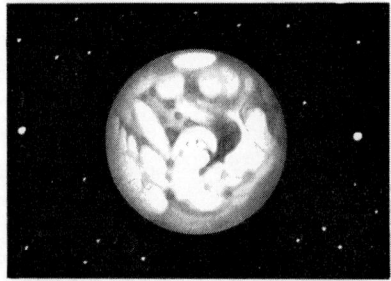

We know Jupiter is a world
that whirls around the sun.
It is bigger than a thousand Earths,
and radio noises come from it,
but nobody knows why.

We know Saturn is a world
that whirls around the sun.
It has bright rings around it
made of bits of rock and dust.

THE SUN

We know Uranus, Neptune, and Pluto
are names of other worlds
that whirl around the sun.
Uranus and Neptune are so far from the sun,
they are probably just giant rocks
wrapped in deep layers of ice.
And Pluto is so far away from Earth
that it can only be seen
through the most powerful telescopes.

URANUS   NEPTUNE   PLUTO

There are probably many other worlds in space,
spinning around other stars,
but they are too far away to see.

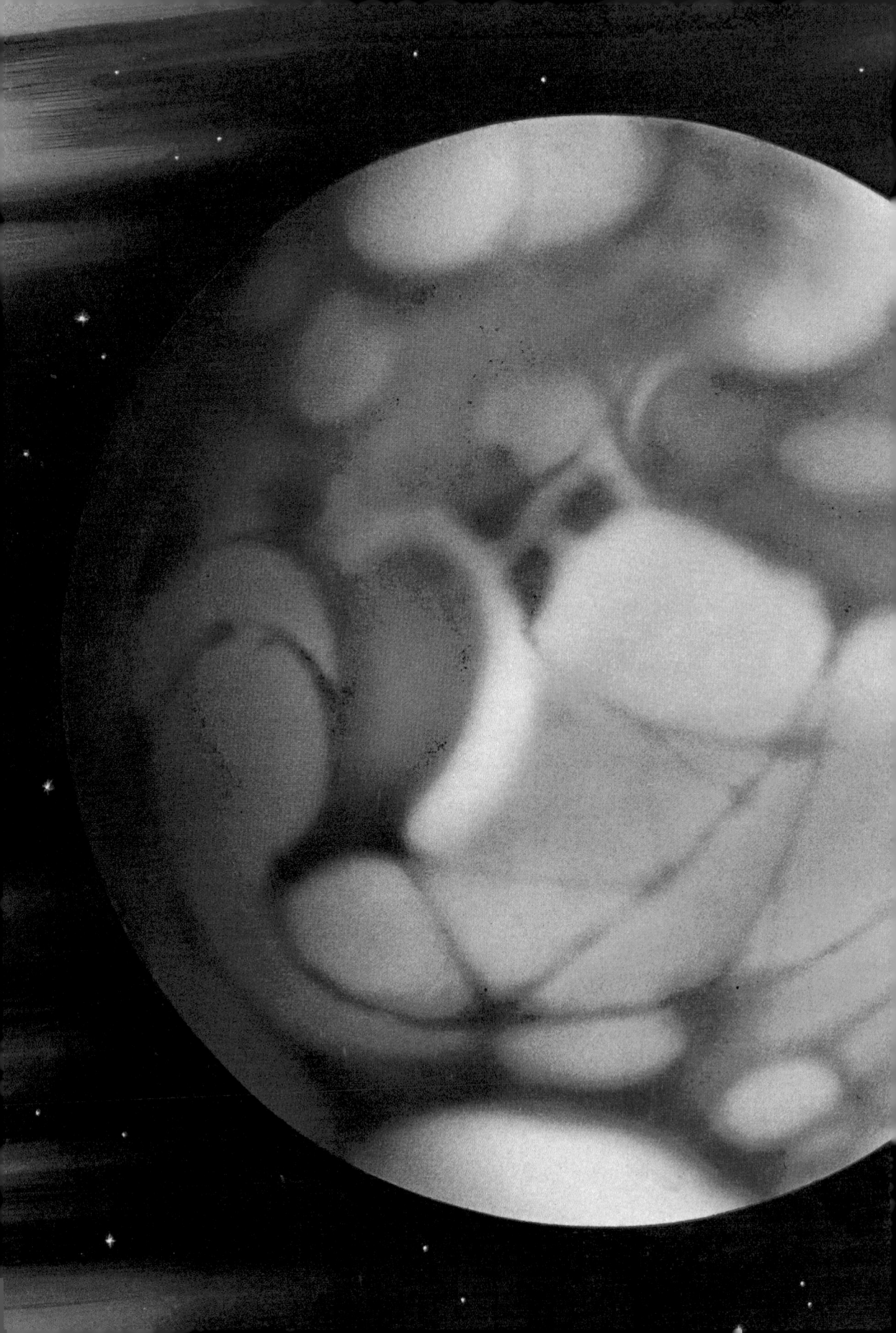

IS SOMEONE
ON MARS?

If you could look at Mars through a telescope,
you would see
patches of white,
and orange,
and fiery red,
mixed with splotches of bluish-green.

People think that these splotches of bluish-green
may be plants.
And where there are plants,
there may be animals.
But it is hard for people on Earth
to know whether there are people on Mars.
So, too, it would be hard for people on Mars
to tell whether there are people on Earth.
All they could see from Mars
would be splotches of blue instead of the sea,
patches of brown instead of the ground,
and wisps of white instead of the clouds.

Someday astronauts may land
on Mars and other planets,
and then we will know for sure
whether there is life on Mars.

MANY MOONS
AROUND OUR SUN

Our moon is not the only moon.
Some of the other planets have moons, too.
Some have one moon.
Some have two moons.
And some have many moons whirling around them.

Pluto and Mercury are planets
that seem to have no moons at all.
But two moons whirl around Mars,
and Neptune has two moons, too—
a tiny one
and a huge one.

Uranus has five moons,
and Saturn has nine.
One of them is bigger than the planet Mercury.

But of all the planets, Jupiter has the most moons.
It has twelve—
midget moons, medium moons, and huge moons.

These are the moons astronomers
have seen whirling around the planets.
But there may be many more moons around the planets
that are too small and too far away to see.

EBEL

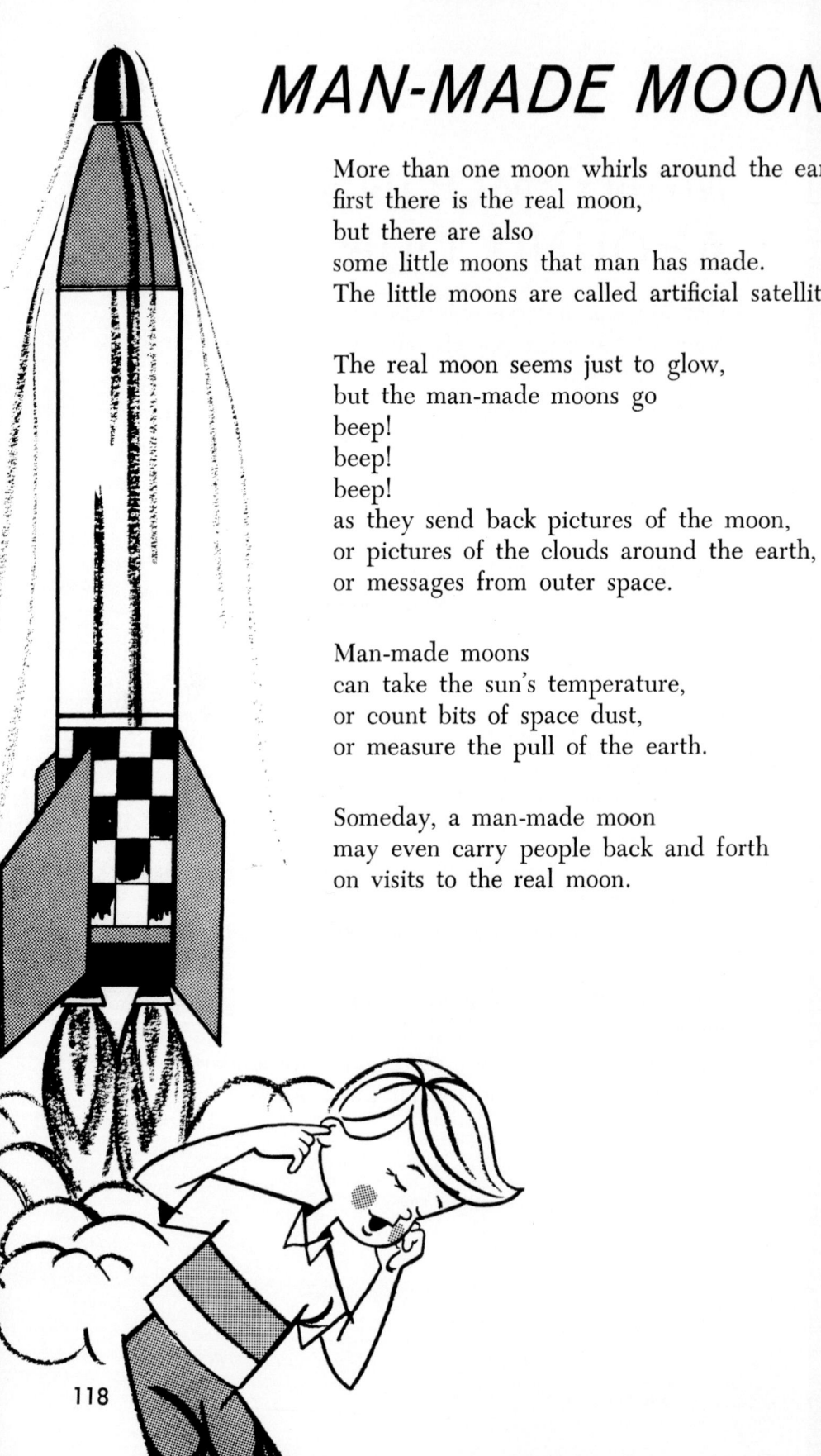

MAN-MADE MOONS

More than one moon whirls around the earth—
first there is the real moon,
but there are also
some little moons that man has made.
The little moons are called artificial satellites.

The real moon seems just to glow,
but the man-made moons go
beep!
beep!
beep!
as they send back pictures of the moon,
or pictures of the clouds around the earth,
or messages from outer space.

Man-made moons
can take the sun's temperature,
or count bits of space dust,
or measure the pull of the earth.

Someday, a man-made moon
may even carry people back and forth
on visits to the real moon.

Storms You

You can hear the rumbling thunder of a coming storm,
and you can see a streak of lightning.
Sometimes, you can even smell rain in the air.
But in outer space,
you can't see, hear,
or smell a storm,
even when it is raging all around you.

Space storms are silent storms of electricity.
There is no lightning to see,
or thunder to hear,
or rain to smell.

Don't See

Space storms make telephones crackle,
radios buzz with static,
television pictures wiggle,
and compass needles jiggle.

But even though the electric storms in outer space
make electric machines do strange things,
they can never hurt you
because the storm is so far away.

PINWHEELS IN SPACE

Space is full of pinwheels—
not tiny paper pinwheels that whirl in a wind,
or firework pinwheels that scatter showers of sparks,
but pinwheels made of billions of stars.
Space pinwheels are called galaxies.

The earth,
the sun,
the moon,
and all the stars you see at night,
are just a part of one galaxy called the Milky Way.

At night,
you can look this way,
or that way,
and all you will see is the Milky Way.

But if you had a telescope,
you could look beyond the Milky Way,
and see many more galaxies
whirling like pinwheels in space,
each with billions and billions of stars.

A pinwheel galaxy of stars
in the nebula of Andromeda

122

JUNK IN ORBIT

There is a lot of junk orbiting in outer space.
Part of the junk is made
of rocks—
rocks as big as houses,
rocks as big as mountains,
and rocks shaped like giant footballs
that tumble,
spin,
and whizz around the sun.
These rocks are called asteroids.

And any rocket ship traveling through space
must be careful not to come too close to
this river of whirling asteroids.

No one knows where this junk came from.
Some people think
that long ago
a big planet burst into thousands of pieces.

Other people think
several small planets crashed into one another
and then burst apart becoming the junk
that orbits the sun.

ROUND AND ROUND WE GO

When you think you are standing still,
you are really spinning around.
You can't feel yourself spinning
because the sky and the clouds and
the trees and the ground
are spinning with you.

The whole earth spins once around each day.
And as it spins,
it whirls around the sun—
once around each year.

But you and the earth are not
the only things that spin in space.
The sun is spinning, too.
The sun,
the earth,
and you whirl together around the center
of a group of stars, called the Milky Way,
which also spins in space.

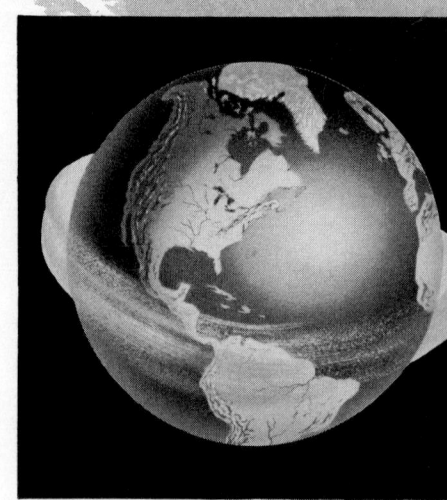

DEEP UNDER

What kind of things are
under the ground you walk on?

"Dirt," you might say, "or rocks."

But there are other things, too.
Exciting and mysterious things...

caves that have never been explored,

caverns filled with stone icicles,

THE GROUND

underground water ponds
no one has ever seen,

gold, silver,
and precious stones
that no one has worn,

and pools of oil
that have not yet been found.

And under the sea there are
mountains that no one has ever climbed.
These are the things
you can read about on the following pages.

129

COULD YOU DIG A HOLE THROUGH THE WORLD?

Have you ever tried to dig a deep hole—
maybe all the way to the other side of the world?
If you used a hand shovel,
you could dig only a few feet.
If you could use a steam shovel,
you could make a hole as deep as a basement.
If you could use a well-digging machine,
you could go down more than three basements deep.
If you could use an oil-drilling machine,
you could dig deeper than a thousand basements.

But to dig to the other side of the world,
you would have to dig much, much deeper!
Of course, no one has ever dug through the world.
The deepest hole ever made is not as deep
as the highest mountain is tall.
And to reach the center of the earth,
you would have to dig a hole
a thousand times deeper than the deepest oil well.

But to dig through the earth,
you would have to dig to the center of the earth
and then all the way out again to the other side of the world.
So when people want to go to the other side of the world,
they usually take a boat
or fly in a plane!

THE DEEPEST HOLE IN THE EARTH
WOULD NOT BE DEEP ENOUGH
TO SHOW ON A MAP OF THE WORLD
THIS SIZE.

WHAT MAKES THE EARTH SHAKE?

What can split the earth,
cause oceans to overflow,
change the course of rivers,
uproot trees,
knock down tall buildings,
and shatter windows for miles around?

An earthquake can do all this
and more, if it is a strong one.
And a big earthquake
rumbles and roars
louder than any thunderstorm.
But most earthquakes are so small
that you can hardly feel them.
And if you did,
you might think it was
just a big truck rumbling by.

Although there are about
a million earthquakes a year,
you may never see, hear, or feel one,
because most earthquakes
happen near oceans
and high mountains.
An earthquake starts
deep in the earth
where the heat from inside the earth
makes the underground rocks
buckle and bend—
the way a piece of bacon
buckles and bends
when you heat it in a skillet.
A big earthquake buckles and bends
the ground so much
that sometimes it
makes big cracks in the earth.

Water Under Your Feet

Where do mud puddles go?
Why do some rivers dry up?
What happens to the water you pour on a sand castle?
The water disappears into the ground
where it fills the tiny holes in the soil
and lines the cracks in rocks.

When it rains, the soil soaks up lots of water
and becomes squushy mud.
The more it rains,
the deeper the water goes into the ground.
In some places,
water can be found more than a mile deep,
even though the land above may be dry and cracked.
Underground water fills the bottom of a well,
and sometimes it pops out of the ground as a spring.

If we live where there is enough water underground,
we can use it
whenever we need it,
even though it hasn't rained for a long time
and the lakes and rivers have dried up.

INSIDE A CAVE

You are deep in a cave and
blackness is all around you.
Dampness is in the air
from the drip-drip-drip of seeping water,
bat wings whir overhead,
lizards scamper across the floor,
and your heart starts beating faster.

Shine a flashlight around,
and you can see monster shadows on the walls,
long spears of stone that look like icicles
hanging from the ceiling,
a bottomless pool just a few steps away,
and a black hole where the cave goes deeper
into the mountain.

Some caves are so big
that they have rooms big enough to hold a house.
And they have underground tunnels
that wind and twist for miles and miles.
But some of the tunnels are so small
you couldn't crawl through them.
Many caves have rivers in them, or once did,
because over the years, underground rivers cut
out the rooms and dug the tunnels to make the cave.

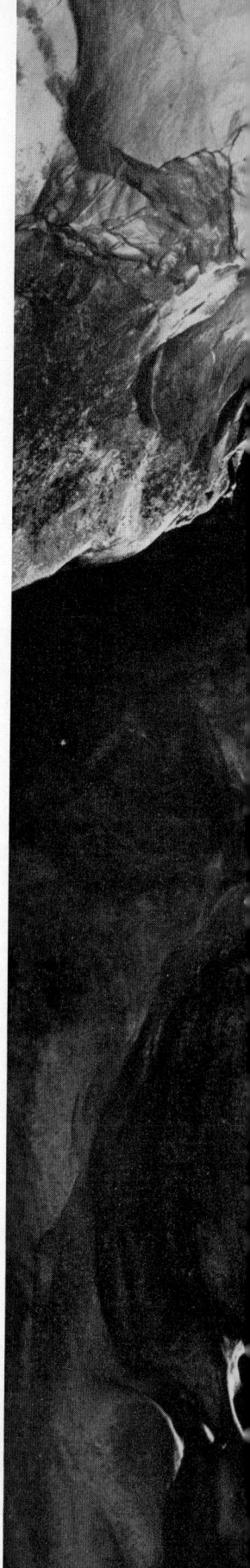

ICICLES IN STONE

Plink, plonk, plink, plonk . . .
water drips in a cave
and makes stone points that look like icicles.
Some points of stone stick up from the floor.
The walls and ceilings of most caves
are made of limestone.
When water drips,
it carries tiny bits of limestone with it.
The waterdrops soon dry up,
but the bits of limestone are left on the floor.
After a long, long time,
and many drops of water,
the bits of limestone grow
into a fat mound called a stalagmite.

Some points of stone
hang down from the ceiling.
Sometimes the water on the ceiling dries
before it has a chance to fall on the floor.
Then the bits of lime
harden on the ceiling as a tiny circle.
Over the years,
more and more circles of lime harden,
one under the other,
until a long "stonecicle"
hangs from the top of the cave.
This "stonecicle" is called a stalactite.

Sometimes stalactites and stalagmites
become so long
that they come together
and make a fat stone pillar
in the middle of the cave.

Manocor cave in Spain
where colored lights reflect
on the rock formations.

MOUNTAINS *under the sea*

Under the sea
mountains are higher,
valleys are deeper,
plains are wider,
cliffs are steeper, and
canyons and gorges are deeper
than they are at any other place on earth.

Undersea mountains have no trees, grass, or snow.
They lie in complete darkness,
never warmed by the sun.

Sometimes the peaks of these mountains
stick out above the water.
Then we call them islands.
But the tops of most undersea mountains lie hidden,
sometimes more than half a mile under the waves.
A few are flat-topped volcanoes that once were islands,
but have been covered by the sea.

Sailors have to know
where the tops of the tallest underwater mountains are
so they won't bump into them with their ships.

WHERE ICE

Did you ever see a boy skating on thin ice?
Unless he was lucky,
the ice cracked,
and he fell into the water.
But you would never break the ice
and fall into the water if you were skating
near the North or South Poles.
There, the biggest elephant,
or the biggest truck,
or a whole railroad train,
would not crack the ice!

NEVER MELTS

Near the North and South Poles,
snow falls the year around,
and it almost never melts.
Snow falls on top of other snow
and packs it down hard to make ice.
So over the years,
the ice gets deeper and deeper.
In fact, in some places
ice can be over a mile deep!

WHERE DOES OIL COME FROM?

The oil that keeps your bicycle from squeaking,
or helps to run your father's car,
or greases your mother's sewing machine,
or heats your house
comes from deep in the ground.
It was made millions and millions of years ago.

Some tiny drops of oil
are almost everywhere deep under the ground,
but the big masses of rock filled with oil are found in the places
that were once, a long, long time ago,
covered by seas and oceans.

In that long ago time, many tiny animals
died in these seas and oceans.
Then sand, rock, and other animals covered them,
and pressed down on them.
After millions of years,
the heat and pressure of the rocks and sand on top of them
turned the sea animals into oil.
People have to drill deep wells through these rocks
to reach the oil.

OIL

ROCKS, SAND, AND SOIL

A rock can be
as hard as steel
or as soft as chalk.

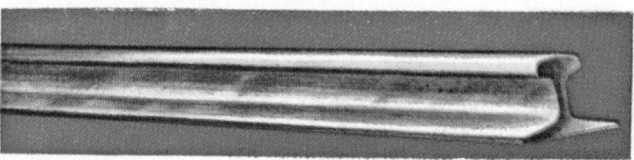

A rock can be made
of millions of tiny pieces
stuck together like a fruitcake,

or a rock can be made
of thin layers
stacked like pancakes.

A rock can be
the colors of the rainbow,

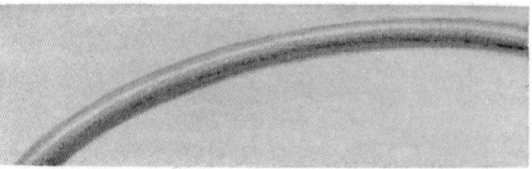

or it can be black,

white,

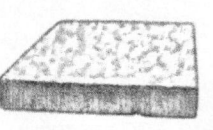

or just plain brown.

A rock can be as shiny
as a Christmas tree light
or as dull as a blackboard.

A rock can be made of gold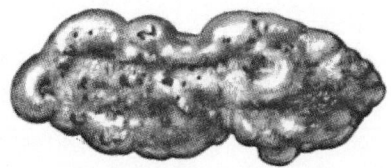

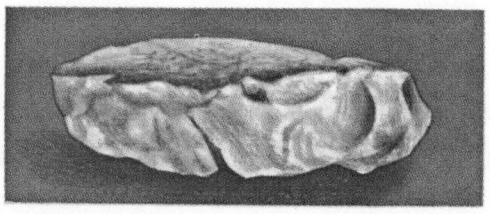

or clay.

A rock can burn up in a second

or not catch fire at all.

A rock can be good to eat,

or it can make you sick.

Rocks are all these things—and more.
On the next pages you will read
about rocks you see every day
and rocks you may never see.

If you had tons and tons of many different minerals
and a boiling volcano about to erupt,
you could make a rock with air bubbles in it—
a rock called pumice.
Pumice is made by fire and heat in a volcano
and is called an igneous rock.

And if you had
tons of broken rock, boulders, cobbles, and pebbles,
lots of wind and rain to break them down into sand,
and a swift-running river to pile the sand in layers,
and a million years to wait,
you could make a layer-cake rock called sandstone.
Sandstone is made of old rocks
that break up into tiny grains of sand
and pile up in layers.
It is called a sedimentary rock.

And if you buried either a sedimentary rock or an igneous rock
under tons and tons of heavy rocks
and heated it with hot gases from deep in the earth,
you could make a rock called marble,
or a rock called slate,
or a rock called gneiss.
Such rocks as these are made
from other rocks by heat and pressure.
They are called metamorphic rocks.

FOR A ROCK

PUMICE

SANDSTONE

MARBLE

GNEISS

SLATE

HUNTING
FOR
GOLD

Look at the pretty stone!
It sparkles bright and yellow in the sun.
It must be . . .
It must be . . .
It must be GOLD!
Is it really gold? How do I find out?

GOLD

You could find out if you took it
to a person who buys gold.
He would test the rock
by heating it over a stove.
If your stone is real gold,
it will not be changed by the heat,
but if your stone starts
to sizzle and smoke, and smell bad,
he will tell you
that your pretty stone is iron pyrite.

Iron pyrite fooled so many gold miners long ago,
that it got the name, "Fool's Gold."
"Fool's Gold" is easy to find.
But real gold is hard to find.
Real gold usually doesn't shine
as brightly as fool's gold.
And it is not usually all in one piece.
Real gold is usually hidden inside
a dull-colored rock in tiny grains or threads.
But save your fool's gold.
Maybe you can fool your friends.

FOOL'S GOLD

A ROCK THAT BURNS

Black coal is a rock made from green plants.
Millions of years ago
strange-looking trees
and giant ferns covered most of the land.
When these big plants died
and fell into swamp mud,
they were soon buried
by other plants that fell on them.

Over the years the dead plants
piled higher and higher
and rotted together to make
a wet, brown mass called peat.
The weight of the water, mud, and sand
mashed the layers of peat flat
and turned them into coal.

Now miners dig the coal out of the ground
so that people can burn it
in furnaces to heat their homes
and make things in factories.

BULLS' EYE AGATE

WEATHERSTONE

PECTOLITE

OPAL

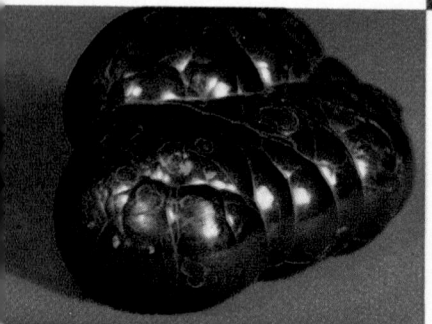

HEMATITE

BARITE

ASBESTOS

154   MALACHITE

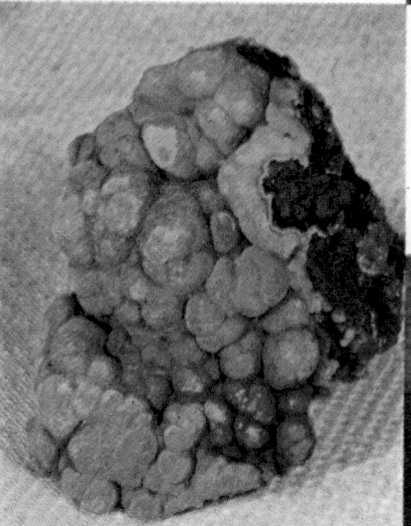

BULLS' EYES AND WEATHERSTONES

Wherever you look,
you can find rocks with beautiful colors and unusual shapes.
Pretty rocks are easy to find.
But if you're lucky,
you might find a gemstone called an opal.
This stone may be black, brown, or white,
but when you hold it to the light,
it flashes the colors of the rainbow.

The "aggie" or "bull's eye" you use in playing marbles
looks like a stone called agate.
You would know an agate
by its beautiful colors, stripes, and spots.

Purple mica is a rock called a weatherstone
because it changes color when the weather changes.
If it is going to rain,
a weatherstone gets damp from the air
and turns a deep purple.
But when the weather is going to be fair,
a weatherstone dries out
and becomes pale gray.
And if you're *very* lucky,
you might find a rock
that looks like a bunch of grapes, called malachite,
a cactus with needles, called pectolite,
a mass of fuzzy strings, called asbestos,
a rose, called barite,
or a large kidney bean, called hematite.

Rocks You Can Taste

If someone at the dinner table said
"Pass the rocks, please,"
what would you give him?
SALT, of course!
Salt is a rock that makes food taste better.
It is found as a mass of big rocks
in salt mines and salt domes.
These big rocks are crushed into tiny rocks
small enough to pass through
the holes of a salt shaker.
Salt also comes
from springs, lakes, and oceans
where it has washed out of rocks.
To get this salt,
water from springs, lakes, and oceans
is poured into shallow pans.
Heat from the sun dries up the water,
and only the salt is left.

SALT MINE

and Smell

Borax is another rock you can taste.
This rock tastes sweet,
and it is used in some toothpastes and soap powders.

Sulfur is a rock known for its bad smell.
This rock smells like rotten eggs.

Another bad-smelling rock is garlic stone (arsenopyrite).
But it smells like garlic
only when it is heated.

BORAX MINE

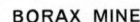

Rocks You Can Wear

The rocks that people wear in rings and necklaces
are not the kind of rocks
you can pick up anywhere.
They are special rocks called gemstones.
They have a pretty color.
They shine in the light.
They are hard to find.
And they do not chip or crack easily.

Gemstones are usually found inside other rocks.
But if you broke open a rock with a gemstone in it,
you might not notice the gem,
because most gemstones are dull-looking
until they are cut, shined, and polished.

But after they are polished,
these dull-looking rocks
may become
beautiful red rubies,

yellow topazes,

blue sapphires,

green emeralds,

purple amethysts,

and blue turquoises.

TREES THAT TURNED TO STONE

Trees can turn into stone!
It is not a fairy's wand that turns them to stone.
It is time that does it—lots of time—
millions and millions of years.
Long, long ago, some trees
fell into a river.
Before they rotted away, as most trees do,
sand and mud covered them.
More and more sand and mud
piled on top of the trees
as the years and years went by.

Under the mud, water with rocks and minerals kept
filling tiny holes and cracks in the wood of the buried trees.
The water also washed away tiny bits of the wood,
and the rocks and minerals took their place.
After a long, long time, all the wood of the trees was gone,
and the rocks and minerals were in its place.
The trees had turned to solid stone!

When the stone trees were uncovered,
people called them "petrified wood!"
Trees that have turned into stone
are found in many parts of the world.
Some of the biggest of them are found
in the Petrified Forest National Park in Arizona.

CROSS SECTION OF
PETRIFIED WOOD

A SHINY BLUE ROCK

One day I found a shiny, blue rock.
It looked like a diamond.
It felt like a diamond.
It just *had* to be a diamond!
But to be sure,
I took my rock to a jeweler.

He looked at it and said,
"What makes you think it's a diamond?"
"See, it's blue and it's shiny.
And it's almost as big as an egg—
just like the one I saw on television," I said.
He said, "Some diamonds are as big as an egg,
but most diamonds are no bigger than a grain of sand."

"But it shines like a diamond," I said.
He said, "Of course, diamonds shine.
But not when you find them.
Diamonds must be cut and polished before they shine."
"But it's blue like the diamond
in my mother's ring," I said.
He said, "Some diamonds are blue.
But diamonds can be yellow, red, green,
brown, or even black."
"But it's hard like a diamond.
I hit it with a hammer, and it didn't break," I said.
He said, "Lots of rocks can't be broken with a hammer.
One way to test a diamond is to try to scratch it with a nail.
Diamonds are so hard that a nail won't scratch them.
In fact, nothing is hard enough to scratch a diamond."

Then he took a nail from a drawer
and scratched it over my pretty blue rock.
The nail made a long, deep scratch.
"Well, I guess I didn't find a diamond after all," I said.

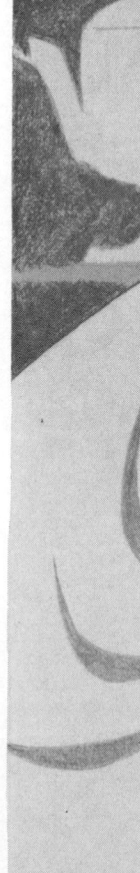

"No," he said. "And it's not likely you'll find one here.
Most diamonds, big or small,
are found in the diamond mines of Africa and Brazil.
Sometimes, though, diamonds are found in parts of America.
Better luck next time."
But I kept my blue rock.
Maybe it wasn't a diamond.
But it looked like one, and it felt like one,
and I wanted to keep it.

THE TINIEST ROCKS

Every grain of sand you ever saw
was once a part of a big rock.
The big rock breaks into a million pieces.
You can't see it happen,
but wind and water
can turn the biggest rock
into a pile of sand.

The wind whistles around the rock
and blows away tiny dust-like grains.
And the grains are sand.

The wind tosses bits of gravel
against the rock
and chips it away bit by bit.
And the bits are sand.

The wind drives raindrops
hard against the rock—
raindrops that knock off chips.
And the chips are sand.

The wind pushes big waves
over rocks in the sea—
waves that roll across the rocks
and carry away tiny pieces.
And the pieces are sand.

Then the waves lift the tiniest
and the shiniest bits of rock,
carry them to shore,
and leave them on the beach—as SAND.

THE BIGGEST ROCKS

How big was the biggest rock you ever saw?
Was it a rock as tall as you,
   a rock you could stand on,
   a rock you could pick up,
   or a rock as big as a mountain?

Long, long ago, the earth was covered with big rocks.
But wind, water, heat, and cold split the big rocks
and broke them into grains of sand,
lumps of clay, loose soil, pebbles,
and rocks of all sizes.

Yet you can still see big rocks
that haven't broken down or worn away—
big rocks of many shapes,
fat boulders,
rugged crags,
steep cliffs,
overhanging ledges,
and high mountains that are all one rock.
Millions of years from now,
these big rocks may break into small rocks and sand, too.

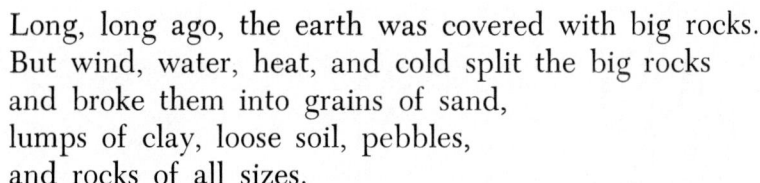

WHAT
IS SOIL
MADE OF?

Did you ever look closely at a handful of dirt?
If you did, you might have seen lumps of clay,
grains of sand,
a pebble or two,
tiny flakes of bright metal,
drops of water,
a broken plant root,
crumbled leaves,
a piece of bark from a tree,
a bone once buried by a dog,
a squirmy red worm,
a scurrying ant,
a sleeping ladybug,
or even an old, rusty nail.

All these things can be found in soil,
along with many plants
and animals too small to see.
If soil were made only of clay, or only of sand,
plants could not grow well in it.
But clay and sand can become rich soil
if water, minerals, dead leaves,
and twigs are mixed with it.
Worms and insects dig holes in soil
and let air in.

Then the soil is rich enough
to grow a field of tall corn,
a garden of green lettuce,
or a grove of tall shade trees.

WIND-BLOWN SOIL

Wind usually wears away
cliffs and hills.
But sometimes it can build them up.

This happens over the years as the wind blows
across dry lands and
dried-up riverbeds.
Dust drifts
and picks up tiny bits
of soft, loose soil
called loess.

During storms and rains,
other winds blow loess into big mounds,
the shape of cliffs and bluffs,
steep slopes,
or slumped hillsides.
Because loess is so loose
and has tiny holes in it,
it will hold water
and keep it packed.

But a lump of loess is so soft
it crumbles into dust
when you press it between your fingers.

171

A TRIP ACROSS

Take a look through these pages
and you will see many things
that you can find
as you travel across the land.

You will walk down a road,
cross over a bridge,

go through a tunnel,

172

THE LAND

and come out in a land
of lakes,

a land of
shifting sand,

a land of canyons,
a land of gorges,

a land of mountains,
a land of cliffs,

a land of rain forests,
or a land of swamps.

WHEN WATER
FILLS UP
A HOLE

Whenever water fills up
big holes,
ditches,
or even valleys,
you have a lake.

And the shape of the lake
is the same
as the shape
of the hole.

You might find a lake
in a mountain,
or in a plain,
or even in a land of swamps.

But all lakes get their water
from rivers,
and from rain.

SALT LAKES

How can salt get into lakes that are far from
the salty ocean?

When rivers and streams flow
over mountains
and through valleys,
the water melts
tiny bits of salt
from the rocks and dirt.

The rivers and streams flow into
other rivers and streams,
or into lakes.
Most often the water flows into the
rivers, streams, and lakes
and then flows out again.
On it goes, and it doesn't stop flowing
until it reaches the salty ocean.

But once in a while,
the water flows into a lake
and doesn't flow out again.
It just stays there.

Then, as the water dries up,
the tiny bits of salt stay
and the lake becomes salty.

That's what happens
in the Great Salt Lake in Utah,
the Dead Sea between Jordan and Israel,
the Red Sea between Arabia and Africa,
and the Caspian Sea between Europe and Asia.

WHEN WATER BUBBLES OVER

Sometimes you can see
water bubbling
out of a rock.
You may think the rock is full of water,
but it's not.
The water comes from a spring
under the rock.

Springs are just underground puddles
of rain water and melted snow
that bubble up from the ground.

At most places water from rain and snow
seeps into the ground.
But at other places
the water can't seep deep into the ground,
because it can't go through the thick underground rocks.
Then the water comes out of the ground
as a spring.

Springs bubble out of the ground
in mountains,
hills, valleys,
or near a cliff or a slope.

Most spring water is cool.
But when water comes from
deep inside the earth,
the spring water may be hot.
These springs are called hot springs.

Sometimes tiny bits of minerals
from underground rocks
mix in the water
and give it a special taste.
These springs are called mineral springs.

FLOWING WELLS

The water you drink or use in the bathtub
may come from a "rock sandwich."

The top and bottom of the sandwich
is made of rock
that water *cannot* go through.
But the filling of the sandwich is made of rock
that water *can* go through.

There are many places where rocks come together like sandwiches.
Some of these "rock sandwiches" are tipped
so that they are higher
at one end than at the other.

When they are tipped,
water from rain and melted snow
seeps through the filling
of the "rock sandwich."
Then it flows down to the lower end
where it collects.

The water collects
until there is so much that it oozes out of the ground.
If a hole is dug here,
the water squirts out of the ground like a fountain.
We call this kind of well an artesian well.
People who live near artesian wells often
get all the water they use from them.

LAND OF SAND

If you stand in a sandy desert,
you will see
sand,
sand,
and more sand
as far as you can see.

In a desert
the sun beats down all day,
and heats the ground.
In a desert
the wind bellows and rages
with little or nothing to stop it.
Sand and dust are blown for many miles.

In a desert
it hardly ever rains ,
so there is very little water.
And there are few plants and animals.

But sometimes you will suddenly see
an island of green in the desert.
This island in a land of sand is called an oasis.
It is a place where water comes out of the earth from
springs or deep wells.
The water gives plants a better chance to grow.

PAINTED DESERT

Imagine a desert that has
sand and rocks
that are
blue,
yellow,
orange,
red,
and purple.

Imagine a desert of
flat-topped mountains,
spindly spires,
and sloping valleys.
Then you know what
the Painted Desert in Arizona or the
colorful deserts in Africa and Asia are like.

How do some deserts get all these colors?
They get them from sandstone and
layers of colored ash
that came from a volcano.
The ash got hard and turned to rock.
Then wind and rain cut and carved
the colored rock.

The colors of the Painted Desert
change during the day
as the sun moves across the sky.
Sometimes the colors are light and bright,
and sometimes they are dark and eerie.

SHIFTING

Wind can blow dirt in your face,
scatter leaves over your yard,
and blow rain and snow against a windowpane.
But did you know
that wind can blow a hill away?

As the wind blows
in some deserts,
it piles the sand
into big mounds, called sand dunes.

But wind does not always blow
in the same direction.
So the sand dunes move
from one place to another as the wind changes.
The wind blows the little grains off the top
of the dune onto the other side.
Those little top grains become
the bottom grains of a new sand dune.
And as long as the wind is blowing,
the dunes keep moving.

In a sandy desert you can tell which way
the wind is blowing
by looking at the sand dunes.
The rounded part of the dune faces the wind.
And the sharp, cliff part is away from the wind.

SAND DUNES

DISAPPEARING

It doesn't often rain on a desert.
But when it does, suddenly a raging river
can appear from nowhere.
The lightning crackles,
the thunder roars,
and the driving rain strikes the hard, dry sand
so fast and furiously
that it begins to run over the ground the way
water runs over a paved road after a hard rain.

Soon the rushing water becomes deeper and deeper
in the gullies and ditches of the desert.
It crashes
and thunders.

RIVERS

It becomes a raging river
that rushes across the desert,
tearing up shrubs
and picking up sand and rocks.

The water sweeps and tumbles along
through the desert
with its load of sand, rocks, and shrubs.
It destroys everything that gets in its way.

But when the rains stop,
the water stops moving.
Quickly it soaks into the sand.
The raging river disappears just as suddenly as it started.

DESERT PICTURES

If you are in the desert,
sometimes you may see
a ship sailing across the sand,
or a mountain of rocks,
or a huge lake of rippling water,
or a clump of palm trees.
But when you walk close to them,
they disappear!
So you know they must be mirages!

A mirage is nothing more than
a picture of a faraway ship,
or a distant mountain, lake, or clump of trees
that is reflected on the sand
by part of the sky.

You do not have to live on a desert
to see a mirage.
Sometimes, when you drive down a paved road
on a hot, summer day,
you may see a mirage
that looks like a puddle of water
190 in front of you.

Photograph of Mirage
in the Sahara Desert

192

WHEN WIND
AND WATER
DIG AND CUT

Pretend the water
from your garden hose is a river.
Let it spatter and trickle on the dirt
in your back yard.
You will see it knock bits of dirt away
to make tiny gullies.

Real rivers do the same thing.
They roll and flow
down mountainsides,
and they cut and carve the ground
into big, sloping valleys,
into craggy cliffs,
into deep ditches,
and into huge gullies.

Wind can cut into mountainsides, too.
The dust and dirt that blows against the rock
chips and carves
bits of the mountain away.
It takes millions and millions of years
for water and wind to cut
and carve away parts of a mountain.

CRACKS IN

With a rumble
and a roar,
a shake
and a quake,
the ground sometimes
spreads apart
into huge cracks
during an earthquake.

These huge cracks are called fissures.

THE EARTH

An earthquake starts deep inside the earth
where heat makes underground rocks buckle and bend.
The ground buckles and bends so much
that it can make huge fissures.

Most earthquakes happen only
near oceans and high mountains.

But the fissures they make can
separate a farmer from his field,
split a street into two parts,
swallow a barn,
and make a river change its course.

CANYONS AND GORGES

Water digs the deepest ditches.
The Grand Canyon is a big ditch.
It is a whole mile deep!
But it was made by a tiny river
that cut and carved
through the ground
for millions and millions of years.

Some canyons are narrow
and have straight sides.
They are called gorges.
These gorges were cut by rivers and streams, too.

NATURAL BRIDGES

Water can build bridges, too.
Sometimes streams push their way slowly
through soft soil and soft rock
underneath a layer of hard rock.
But the water doesn't cut the hard rock, so
a bridge of stone is left.

STRAIGHT UP A CLIFF

Barber poles are striped.
Candy canes are striped.
And many cliffs are striped, too.
The stripes may be
red,
yellow,
white,
blue,
black,
or gray.
Sometimes you may see them when they look
like a stack of colored pancakes.

Long ago, the sea piled
layers of red clay,
yellow sand,
white chalk,
and blue, gray, and black mud
on top of each other.
The layers were pressed and squeezed together
into layers of rock,
after millions and millions of years.

Sometimes land shifts and earthquakes push parts of the land
up in the air. These parts become cliffs.
You can see the rock layers in the cliffs.

ICY BULLDOZERS

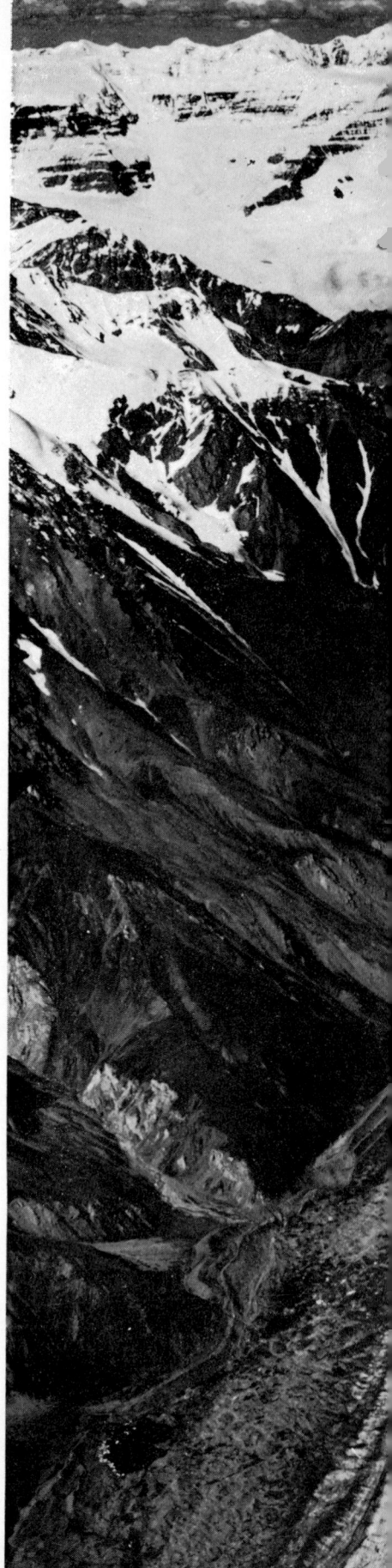

Imagine a huge river
moving slower than a turtle
from the top of a mountain
to the bottom.
There are such rivers, but they are
not rivers of water, like the ones you know.
They are rivers of ice called glaciers.

Glaciers are made of snow
that is pressed and squeezed together.

They move inch by inch
down mountainsides,
picking up rocks and dirt
and making deep valleys,
narrow ridges, and mounds.

As snow falls on the top of a mountain,
the weight of the new snow and ice
squeezes out the old ice,
just as peanut butter and jelly
in a sandwich
can be squeezed out
from between the slices of bread.

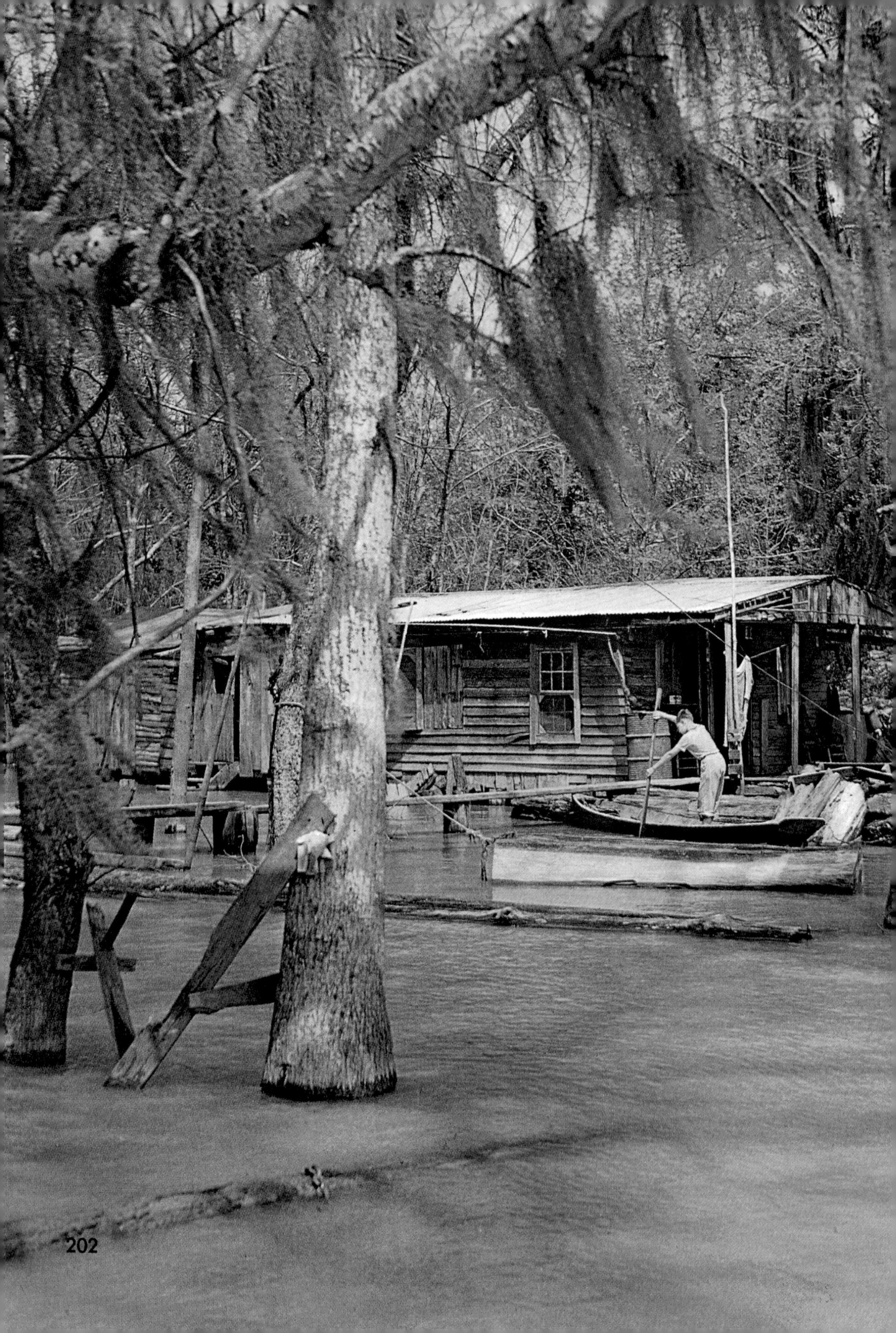

land of mud and muck

If you tried to walk through a swamp,
the mud might soon be up to your knees.

If you tried to paddle
a boat through a swamp,
the oars might get tangled
in the weeds and the vines.

In a swamp there are
a few patches of dry land.
Water, mud, and muck
are all around you.
Weeds grow tall
in the muddy water.

In some swamps
strangely twisted and stunted trees grow,
moss hangs from the tree branches,
and huge water lilies float on the water.

In some swamps
otters tumble and splash,
alligators sleep and yawn,
water snakes creep and slide,
and many other animals move around.

RAIN FORESTS

If you walk through a rain forest,
the drip, drip, drip
from water-soaked leaves after a rain
will splatter on your head, arms, and hands.
Rain forests are found where it is very hot
and sometimes where it is not very hot.

In a rain forest it is dark
because little sunlight
can get through the thick covering of the treetops.

In a rain forest the trees are taller
than most trees you usually see.
And they have big leaves
that fall and cover the ground.
Some bushes in the forest may grow as tall as trees.

In a rain forest
the climbing plants are twined and tangled
around most tree branches.
And sometimes the tangle of creepers and vines
is so thick on the ground that you cannot walk!

In a rain forest where it is hot
snakes slither, turtles creep,
birds chirp, monkeys chatter,
and many other animals move around quickly.
In a rain forest where it is not hot,
squirrels scamper through the trees
and lizards crawl along the ground.

Things grow so well in a rain forest
because it is wet—
very wet.

Rain forest near Olympia, Washington

WHAT IS QUICKSAND?

Quicksand is a fine, soft sand,
wet with water.
It can swallow a pig,
or a man, or even
an elephant.

If you step into quicksand,
you will slowly sink up to your knees.
If you thrash and squirm,
you will sink deeper and deeper.
But if you lie flat on your back
with your arms stretched out,
you can float on the sand,
as you can float on water.

If you have a pole, you can
wiggle it under your shoulders
all the way down to your legs.
Then you can pull your legs up and out
of the sand.
Then you can look around
for the shortest way out of the quicksand
to solid ground, and start rolling toward it.
Between rolls, you can rest on your back
with your arms stretched out.
Otherwise, you might sink into the sand again.

WHERE AM I?

How do you know which way to go when you travel?

Do you look at the sun to find your way?

You can, if you know where to look.

Do you look at the stars to find your way?

You can, if you know where to look.

Do you look at a compass to find your way?

You can, if you know where the needle points.

Do you look at a picture map
to find your way?

You can, if you know
what the pictures mean.

Do you look at a road map
to find your way?

You can, if you know
what the lines and numbers mean.

Look through the next few pages.
Then you will know
how to find your way
by the sun, by the stars,
by a compass, and by maps.

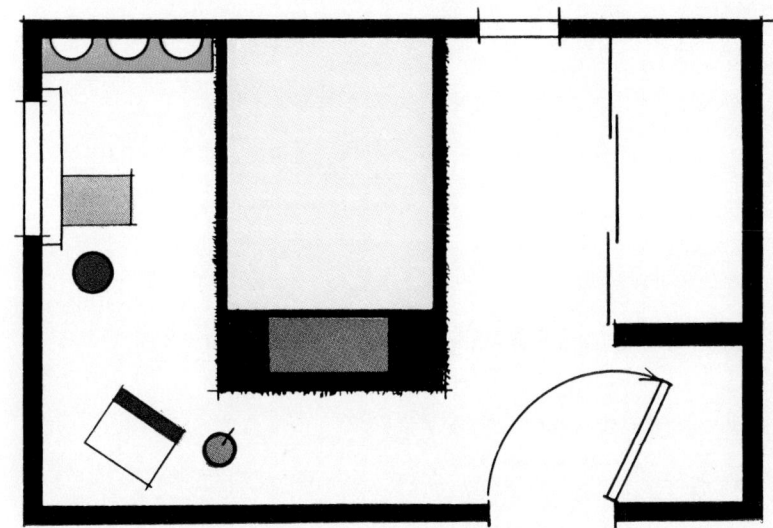

A MAP OF YOUR ROOM

You can draw a picture of your room two different ways.
One way is
to sit in your room
and draw whatever you see.

The other way is to pretend
that you are looking down
through a hole in the ceiling.
This way you can draw
all four walls,
show where the door is,
and show the top of all the things in your room.

The first drawing is just a picture of your room.
But the other drawing is a map.

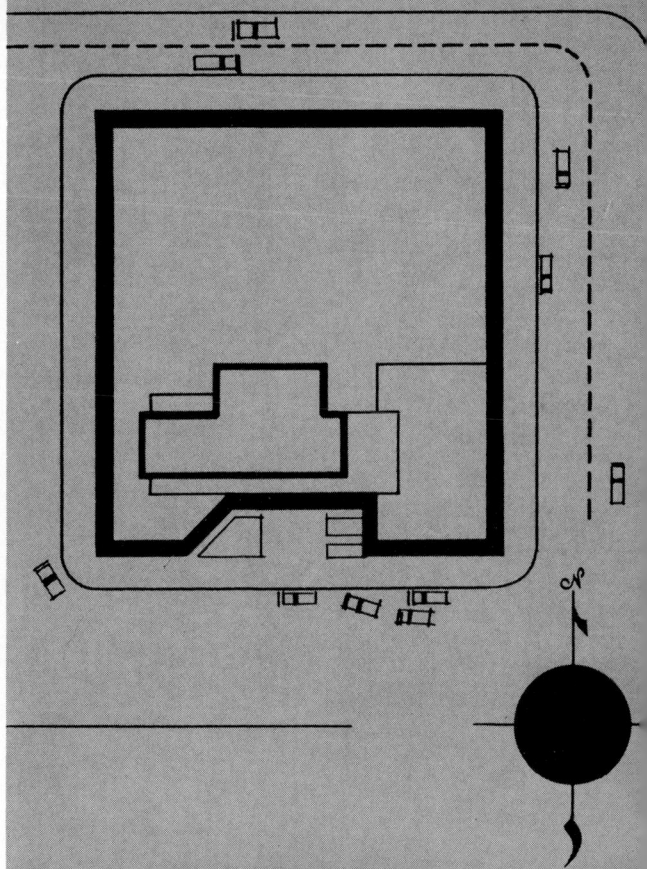

THE TOP OF THINGS

If you are standing on the street looking
at a building,
you will see the side,
but never the top!

And if you are in a helicopter
flying over the building,
you will see
a bit of the side
and most of the top.

And if you are looking at a map
of the same building,
you will not see the sides.
You will see only the top,
because a map shows the top of things.

How buildings would look
if you were on the street.

If you are standing on a street in a city,
you can see the street
and the things around you.
But you cannot see far enough to know
where the street you are standing on
comes from
or where it goes.

Where Do the Streets Go?

How buildings would look
if you were in a helicopter.

If you are looking down from a tall building,
you can see several streets in the city.
But you still will not be able
to see far enough to tell
where the streets come from
or where they go.

If you have a map of the city, you can see all the streets.
And the map will help you see
where the streets come from and where they go.

The splotches of color on this map show where to find
the buildings in the pictures on the facing page.

Adapted courtesy
Rand McNally & Co.

216

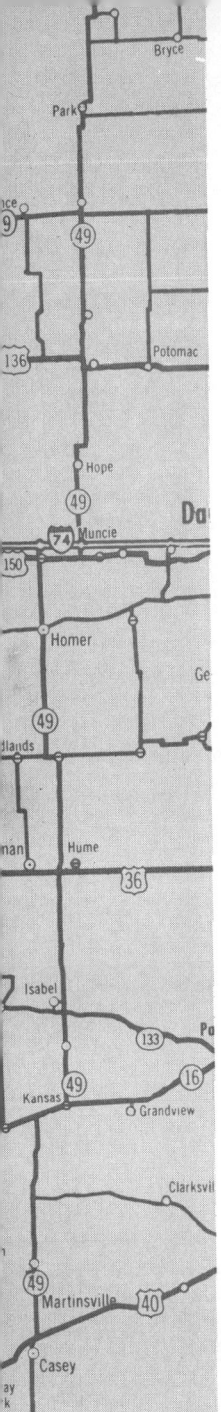

LINE AND NUMBER MAPS

The squiggly lines and numbers on a road map—
the kind you can get at a gas station—
can show you ways to get from place to place.

The squiggly lines are roads.
Thin squiggly lines are smaller roads.
Fat squiggly lines are highways.

Towns, cities, and other places to visit
are usually tiny circles
that have names of places printed next to them.

HOW TO USE
A ROAD MAP

Look for the town of Springfield on this map.
Now look for Decatur.
Which road would you take to go
from Springfield to Decatur?

Now find Champaign.
Which road would you take
from Decatur to Champaign?

If you follow the lines and numbers,
you can find your way from place to place.

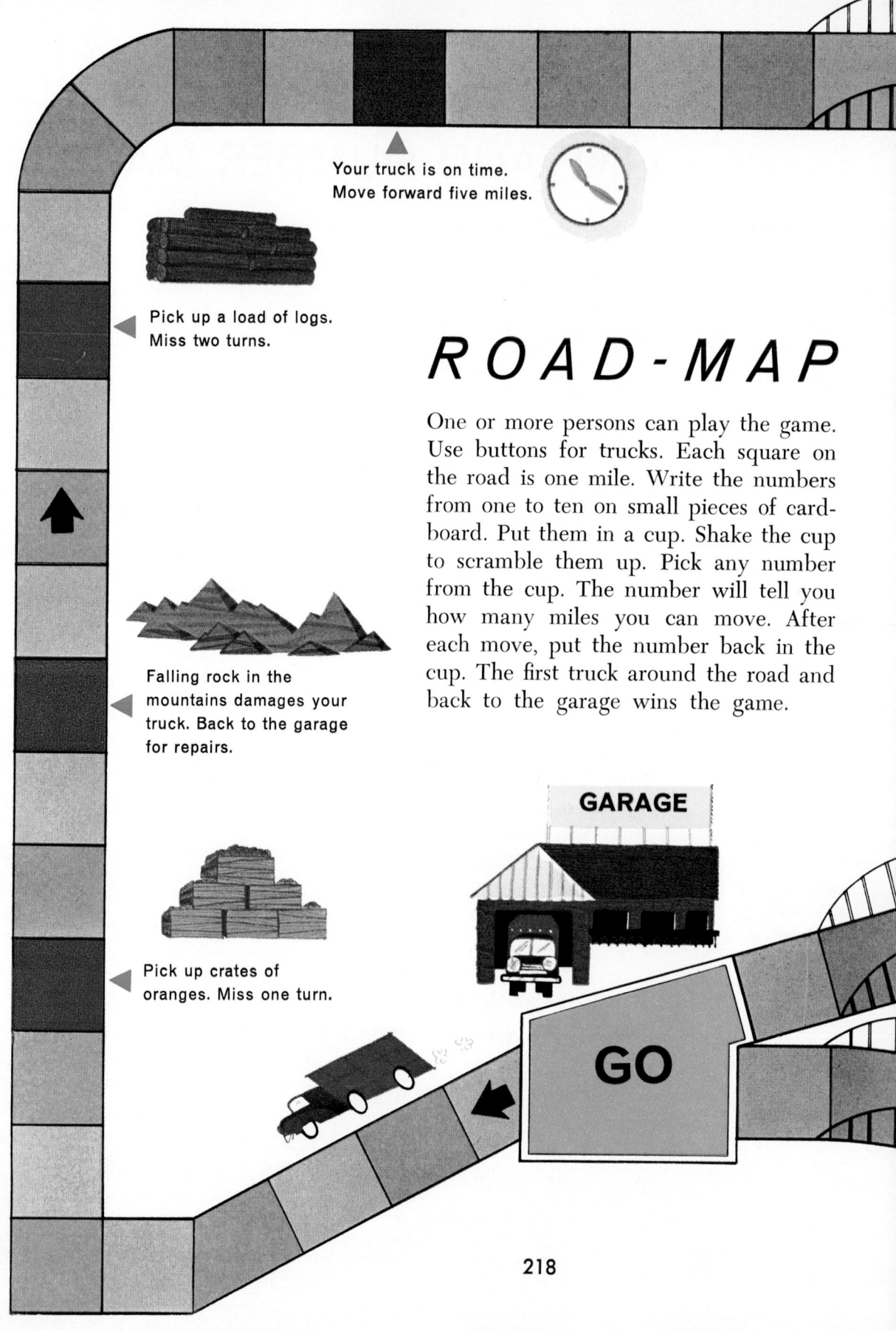

Your truck is on time.
Move forward five miles.

Pick up a load of logs.
Miss two turns.

ROAD-MAP

One or more persons can play the game. Use buttons for trucks. Each square on the road is one mile. Write the numbers from one to ten on small pieces of cardboard. Put them in a cup. Shake the cup to scramble them up. Pick any number from the cup. The number will tell you how many miles you can move. After each move, put the number back in the cup. The first truck around the road and back to the garage wins the game.

Falling rock in the mountains damages your truck. Back to the garage for repairs.

GARAGE

Pick up crates of oranges. Miss one turn.

GO

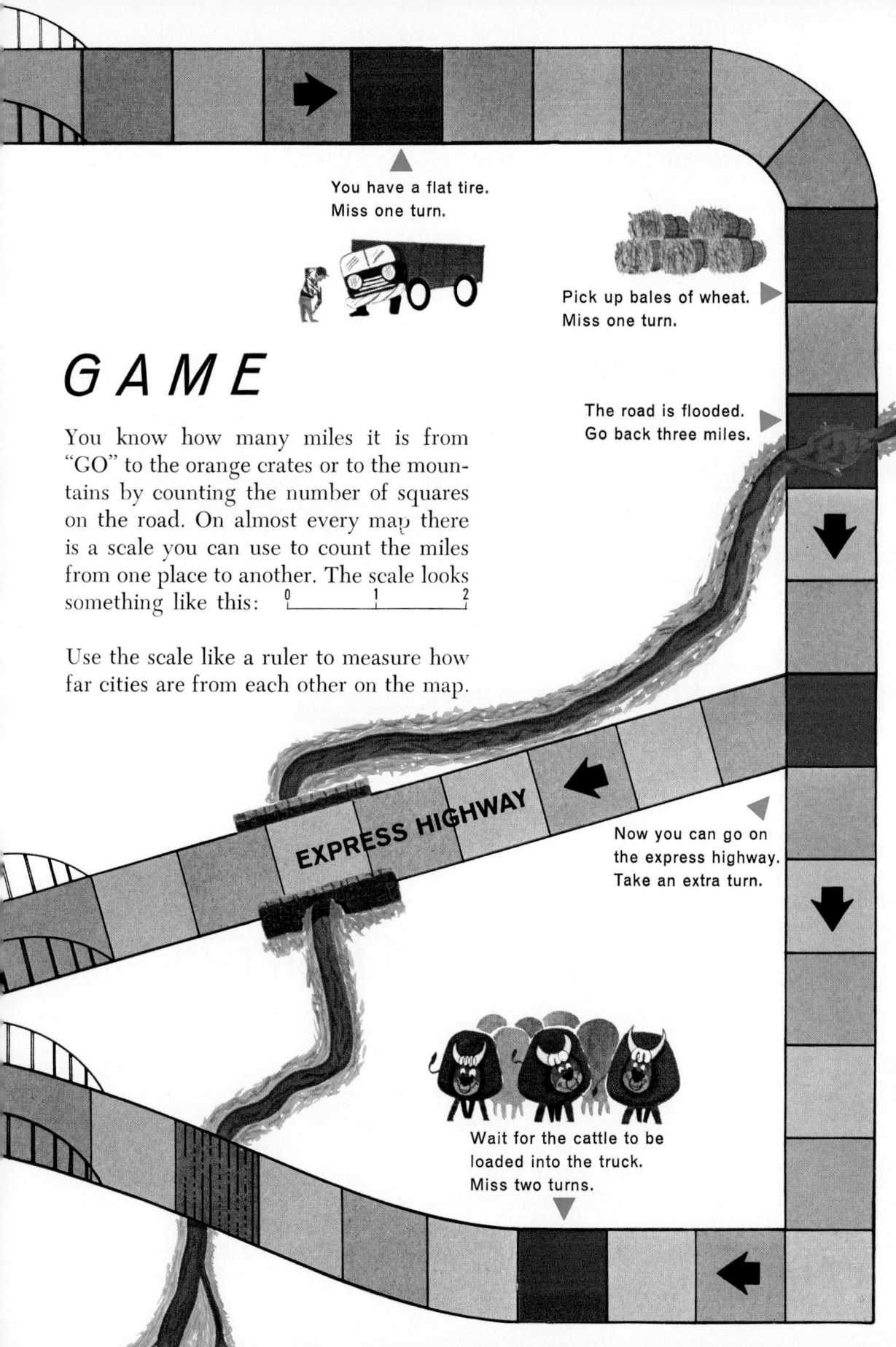

You have a flat tire.
Miss one turn.

Pick up bales of wheat.
Miss one turn.

The road is flooded.
Go back three miles.

GAME

You know how many miles it is from "GO" to the orange crates or to the mountains by counting the number of squares on the road. On almost every map there is a scale you can use to count the miles from one place to another. The scale looks something like this: 0 — 1 — 2

Use the scale like a ruler to measure how far cities are from each other on the map.

EXPRESS HIGHWAY

Now you can go on the express highway. Take an extra turn.

Wait for the cattle to be loaded into the truck. Miss two turns.

WHICH WAY IS NORTH?

If you know which direction north is,
you can always find your way.
If you don't know where north is,
you can find out by looking at a shadow.
Put a stick in the ground
at noon on a sunny day
and look at the stick's shadow.
If you live north of the equator,
the shadow will always point north.

Another way to tell the direction of north is to
look at the stars on a clear night
and find the Big Dipper.
The two end stars in the bowl of the dipper
are called "pointers."
They point to the North Star.
And the North Star is always in the northern part of the sky.

But the easiest way to find north
is by using a compass.
Turn to the next page to find out
how to use a compass.

ALWAYS pointing north

If you have a compass,
you do not have to wait
for a sunny day
or a starry night
to find out
which way is north.

The North Pole is like a magnet,
and a compass pointer is pulled toward it.
So the pointer of a compass always points north.

MAKE YOUR OWN COMPASS

You can make your own compass
if you have a piece of cork,
a magnet, and a sewing needle.
Float the cork in a cup of water.
Stroke the sewing needle against the magnet five or six times
so that it will be magnetized.
Be sure to stroke it in the same direction each time,
and not back and forth.
Then lay the needle on the floating cork.
The needle will turn so that one end
will always point to the north.

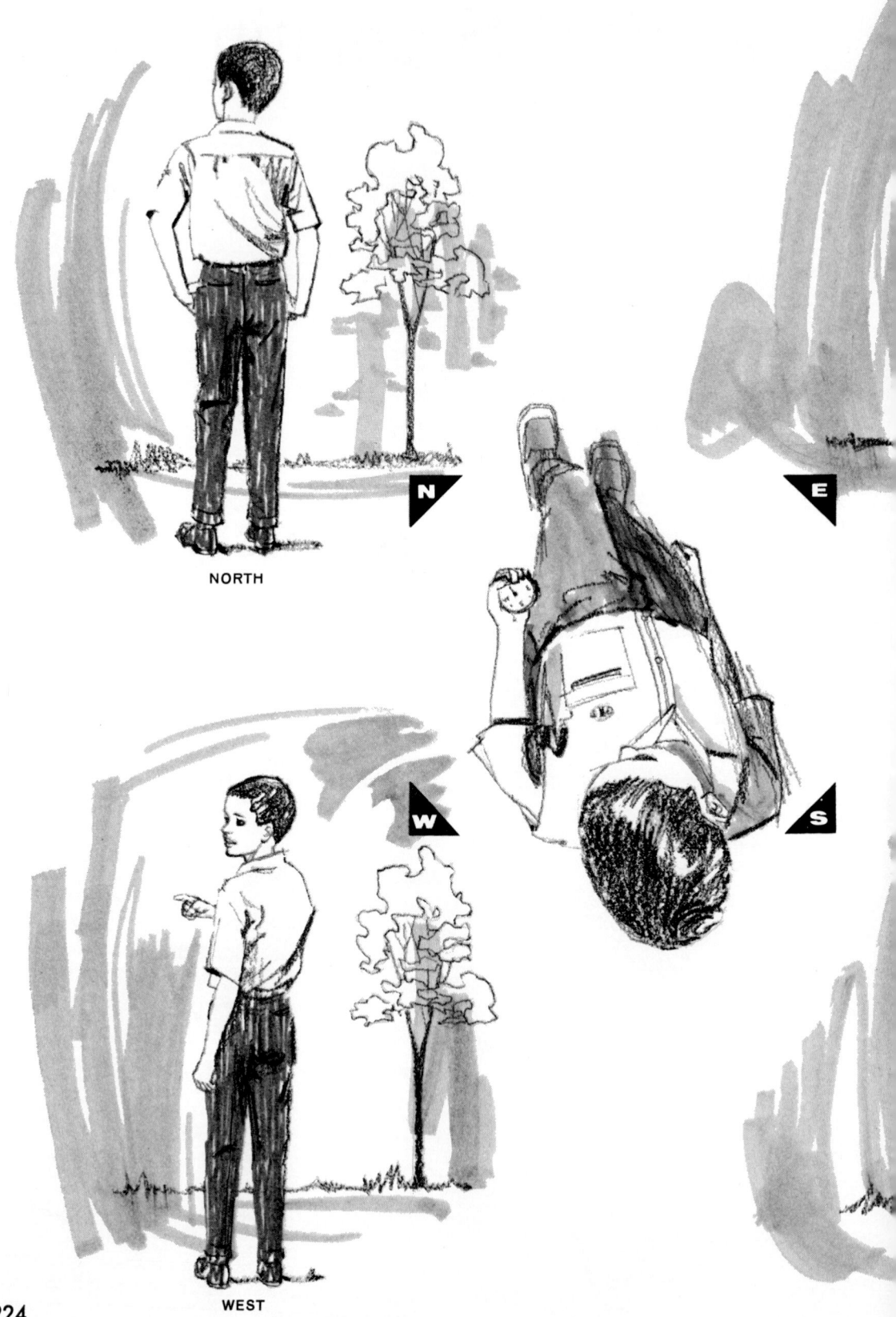

NORTH

WEST

EAST

WHERE ARE SOUTH, EAST, AND WEST?

The shadow of a stick,
the North Star,
or a compass
can tell you which way is north.
But how do you find which way is
south,
east,
or west?

All you do is find out where north is.
Then when you know
that you are facing north,
the direction behind you will be south.
The direction on your left will be west.
And the direction on your right will be east.

So if you know which way north is,
you can find all the other directions.

SOUTH

a pirate map

Suppose you found this pirate map
in an old, dusty trunk.
How would you find the buried treasure?
The pictures on the map
will help you find the way to the treasure.

POINTS OF COMPASS—show you which way is north,
south, east, and west

 BLACK PATCH BEACH—where you must watch out
for quicksand

PIRATE'S COVE—where you can land on the island

BOTTOMLESS LAKE—where there is no way to cross

 BARRIER REEF—where you have to take the long way around

TABLE ROCK—a good place to stop and rest

 SPYGLASS MOUNTAIN—where you can look out over
most of the island

LOST FOREST—where you can't get through

NEEDLE ROCK—something you have to go around

DEAD MAN'S CAVE—where there is an arrow
pointing the way

ALL KINDS OF MAPS

Picture maps, treasure maps, and road maps
are on flat paper.
But some maps are like big balls,
and some maps are bumpy.

The map that is like a ball is called a globe.
It is a round map shaped like the earth.
When you spin the globe,
you can see all the countries
and oceans of the world on it.

Some maps have bumps for mountains
and dents for lakes and valleys.

But there are other kinds of maps, too.

A sailor uses a special kind of map,
called a chart,
that tells him
how deep the water is,
where sand bars and other dangers are,
what the shore of the land looks like,
and where he can dock his boat.

An airplane pilot uses a chart
that tells him
where the airports are,
where the lakes and rivers are,
how high mountains are,
and how high he should fly.

PILOT'S CHART   SAILOR'S CHART

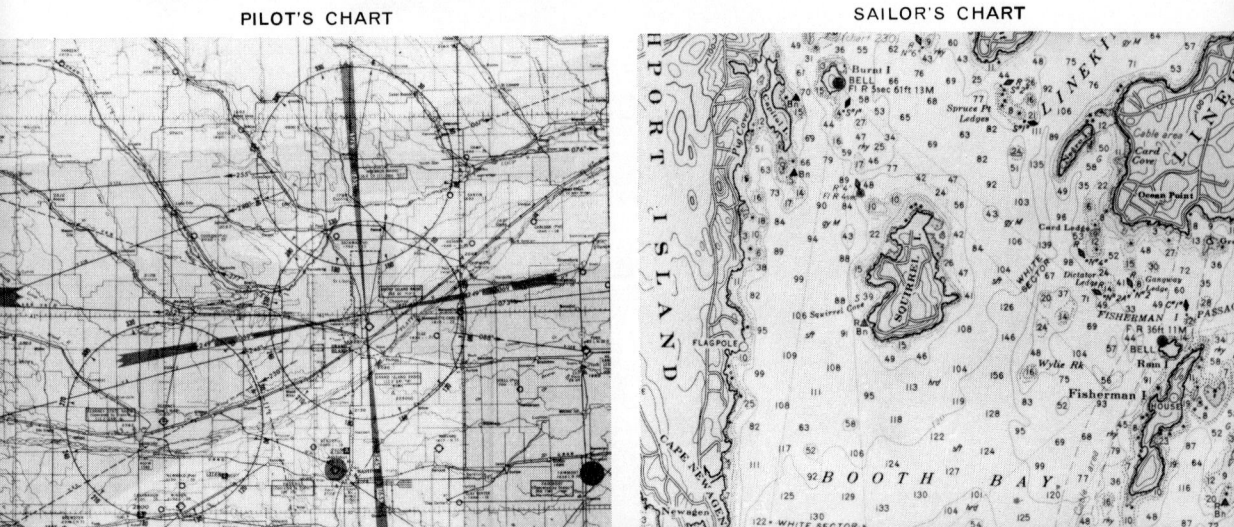

A TRIP AT SEA

Sometimes I pretend I am
the captain of a ship
setting out from a secret cove.
And the only one to see me sail away
is the keeper of a lighthouse
high above me on a cliff.

There are times
when the sea is so calm
my ship lies still,
and I pace the deck
wishing a wind would blow.

But sometimes the sea is so rough
my crew must lash me to a mast
so the waves won't wash me overboard.

Far out in the ocean
I see all sorts of things float by—
orange crates,
sleeping seagulls,
and great chunks of ice called icebergs.

I have even seen a seaweed sea.
I wonder if monsters live there.

So, if you want to go to sea,
look through the next few pages
to find out what the sea is like.

WHERE DOES THE

The ocean may have a top of rippling whitecaps
or towering waves of water.
The ocean has a bottom of deep craters
and high mountains.
But does it have a beginning?
Does the ocean begin at your toes,
when you let it gurgle around your feet at a beach?
Or does the ocean begin where it pounds
against the cliffs of a far-off land?

OCEAN BEGIN?

Does the ocean begin under the ice at the top of the world,
or does it begin under the sun of the southern seas?
The ocean begins and ends
wherever it meets the land.
It spreads between the lands of the world,
or gleams in a sunlit harbor,
or surges as surf onto the beach of a cove.

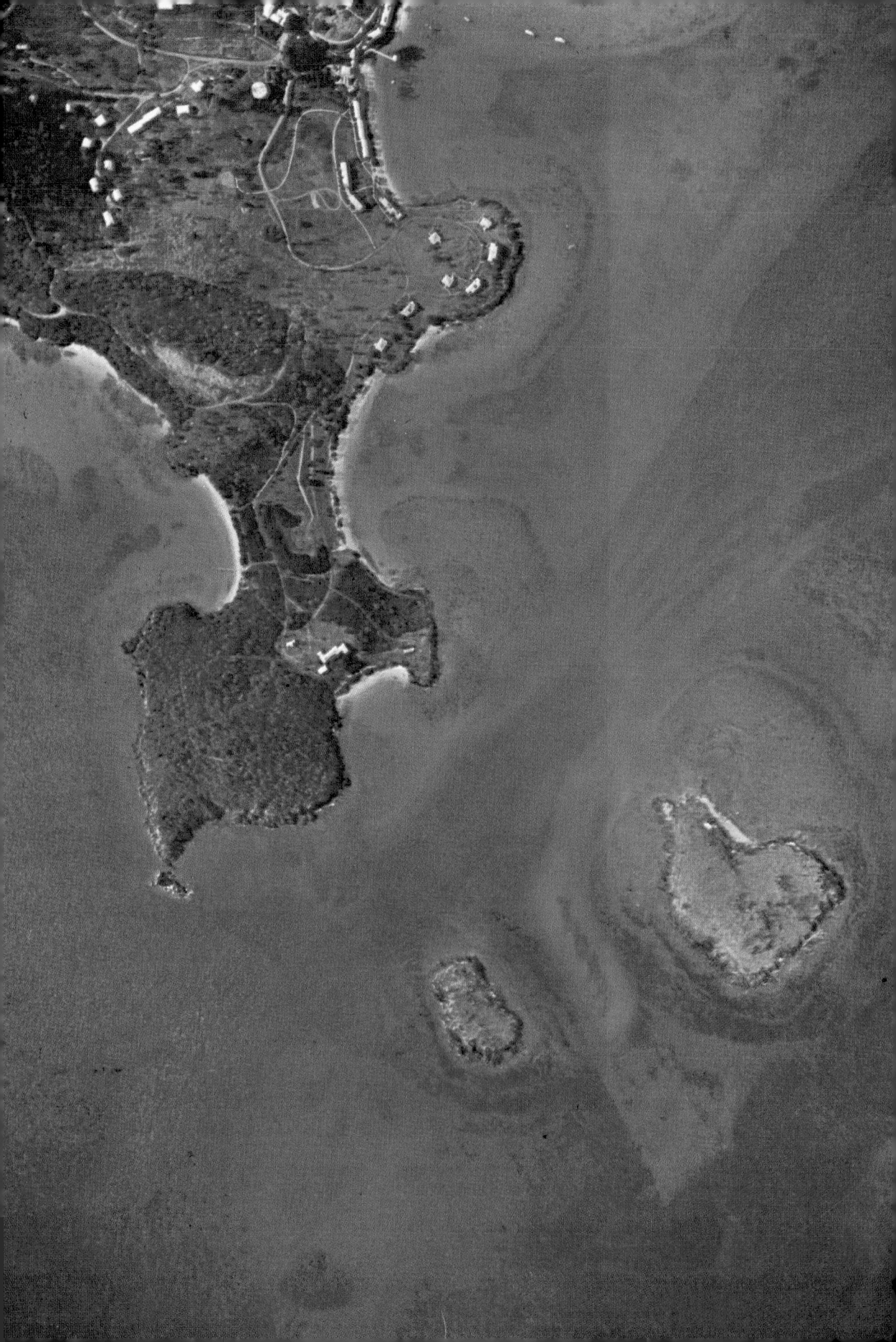

COLORS OF THE SEA

The surf at the seaside has no color at all.
It's just a swirling mass of colorless bubbles.
But if you look beyond the surf,
where the water gets deep,
the sea appears to be blue,
or green,
or gray,
or even black with streaks of silver.

Where the water is too deep
to see the bottom of the sea,
the water acts as a mirror
and reflects the sky.
It reflects the brilliant blue of a summer sky,
the gray or green of a stormy sky,
and even the black and moonlit sky of night.

Aerial photograph
of ocean and peninsula.

THINGS THAT FLOAT

You can find almost anything floating in the sea.
You might find a coconut,
or a half-filled water keg,
or a twisted tree branch from a faraway island.

You might find a seaman's hat,
or an abandoned raft,
or a wicker chair with a missing seat.

You might find a shoe with a hole in the sole,
or a rag doll without a head,
or a life preserver from the good ship *Mirabella*.

236

IN THE SEA

A tattered sail,
an old pair of pants,
waterlogged pages of a book,
an old sea chest,
or a big red balloon,
are all things you might find floating in the sea.

And if you are lucky,
you might find a bottle with a message sealed inside it
bobbing on the waves.

The sand on a beach is always moving.
Sometimes you can see it move
as it trickles and fills up your footprints,
or crumbles and makes part of your sand castle fall down.
But most of the sand on a beach moves too slowly to see.
The tiny grains of sand,
blown by the wind,
tumble and roll
or swirl and shift from place to place
in the surf of the sea.

And as the sand moves,
the beach changes.
It can change from a beach covered with ripples
to a beach that is flat and smooth.
A beach can be broad one day,
and narrow the next,
as mounds of sand pile up where the sea used to swirl.

WHAT IS A BAY?

A bay is a place where the sea laps
at the beach with gentle waves
and a breeze smells of seaweed.
It is a place of musty caves,
shrieking seagulls,
and boats pulled up on the beach.
A bay is a place to climb among rocks,
search for crabs,
or step on seashells half-buried in the sand.
A bay is a place where ships sway at anchor
and bell buoys clank in the distance.

Even though the water outside the bay
rages and storms,
the water inside the bay stays calm,
because a bay
is just a part of the sea
that is nestled
and protected by land on each side of it.

Photograph of a bay taken from an airplane.

241

SHALLOW SPOTS
AT SEA

The ocean is deep.
But there are places
where you can sit with water up to your waist
and shout to ships that go sailing past.
These places are called sand bars.

A sand bar is sand that is piled
and heaped,
swept
and pushed,
squeezed
and rolled,
and shoveled by the waves of the sea
until it becomes
a giant underwater sand hill far out from shore.

Sand bars may be fun to sit on,
but they are dangerous for ships.
Sailors have to know where the sand bars are
so they can steer their ships around them.

What Is an Island?

The top of a mountain
is usually called a peak.
But the top of a mountain that is mostly under water
is called an island.

Sometimes islands rise up from the bottom of the sea.
Deep down, the ground shakes.
Then it splits and spews up
rock so hot it makes the sea boil and bubble.
The hot rock
piles up and up
until a mountain bursts from the sea
in clouds of steam.

Then, still belching smoke and molten rock,
the mountain rises higher and higher above the water.
The rumbling
and the flow of molten rock finally stops.
The top of the mountain has become a new island
in the middle of the ocean.

There are other kinds of islands, too.
Some islands are small pieces of land
separated from big pieces of land by the ocean.

A LIGHT THROUGH THE NIGHT

When sailors
sail their ship through a stormy night,
they squint through the stinging spray
and search the sea for a light.

The light they look for
is a lighthouse light.
It may blink from the top of a cliff,
or shine from a tiny island,
or wink from a perch of steel girders.

But when sailors see the light shine through the night,
they know that land is dangerously near.
They may be sailing close to shoals,
or sand bars,
or rocks and reefs.
Then a ship may run aground
and be smashed to pieces
by the waves of the stormy sea.

ABOVE THE TOP

When you pour out a bucket of sand,
you get a mound of sand on the ground.
But if you pour out a bucket of water,
you do not get a mound of water.
All you get is a puddle.

As you pour the water,
it streams
and trickles about
until it fills the lowest places on the ground around you.
It is just the same with the water in the ocean.
The ocean has spread out.

OF THE OCEAN

It surges
and flows,
and fills most of the low spots all over the earth.
But parts of the land are so high,
there is not enough water in the ocean to cover them.

This is where people live,
and they can measure how high the land is
above the top of the ocean.
They say that a mountain,
or a hill,
or a desert
is a certain number of feet above the top of the ocean—
or above "sea level."

249

An Iceberg

in Your Hands

An iceberg may be as large as a house,
or as wide as a meadow,
or as tall as a mountain.
But there comes a time
when you can hold an iceberg in your hands.

An iceberg is a giant chunk of ice
that breaks off a glacier at the North or South Pole.
It tumbles into the water
with a noise like rumbling thunder
and then drifts out into the ocean.
On and on it drifts—
away from the cold arctic water
and into warmer seas.

Then the iceberg begins to melt.
It gets smaller
and smaller
and smaller,
until it is small enough to hold in your hands.

A TIDAL WAVE

When you sit in the surf on a beach,
waves can bubble around your toes,
or they can lift you up
and plunk you down again.

With a roar that hurts your ears,
one kind of wave can burst upon a beach
and smash a tree as if it were a matchstick.
It is called a tidal wave—
a wave of dark, green water
that towers so high it seems to hide the sky.

A tidal wave starts
when an earthquake makes the ground shake
under the sea.
The waves churn
and swell
and mingle
until they become one huge tidal wave
that roars toward the shore.
It bursts over the land,
smashing everything in its way.

Then, as suddenly as it appeared,
the tidal wave is gone,
and the water sweeps and swirls back into the sea.

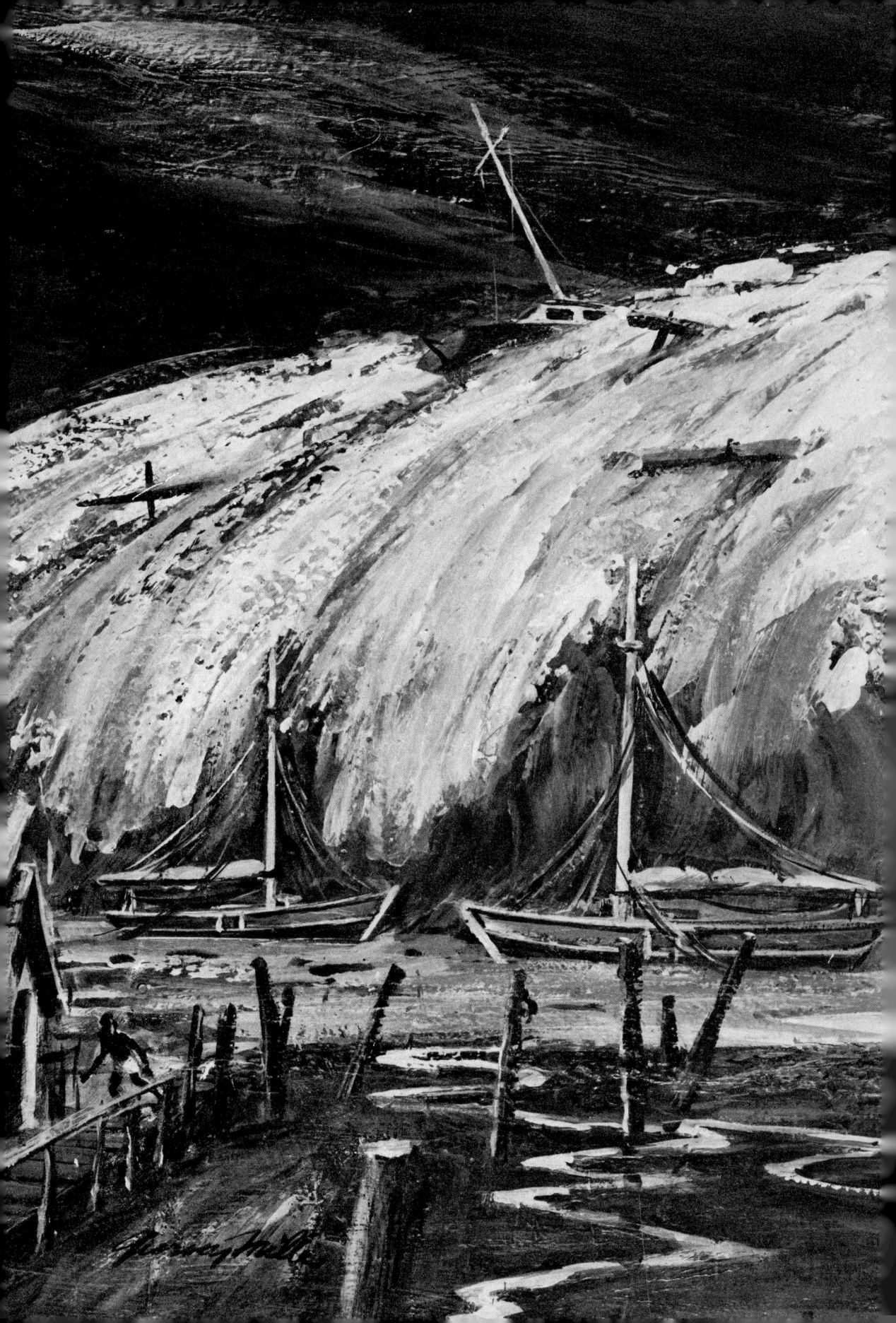

THE SEAWEED SEA

Way out in the ocean,
there is a place
where the wind seldom blows
and the water is warm and still.
It is called the Sargasso Sea.

Great ocean currents
swirl
and sweep
around it.
The currents bring seaweed
that fills the Sargasso Sea,
until it is a thick seaweed sea.

Long ago, when all big ships had sails,
sailors thought that monsters lurked
beneath the water of this sea
and that any ship that went there
would get
trapped in the seaweed,
never to be seen again.
But sailors today know this is not true.

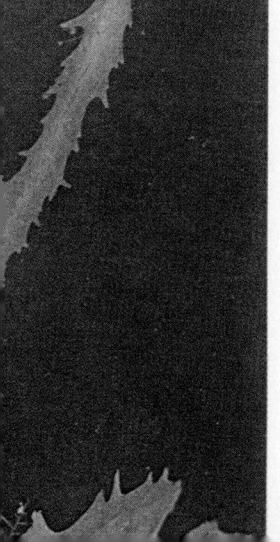

A sargassum fish swims through
the seaweed of the Sargasso Sea.

The Many Moods of the Sea

Sometimes the sea seems to be in a playful mood.
It gurgles and foams
as it swirls around your feet
and tickles your toes.
A playful sea is a gentle sea
that plops and smacks against a boat
as it glides through the water.
A playful sea is a clear, bright sea—
so bright it can mirror you when you fish from a pier,
and so bright it looks clean enough to drink—
even though it is much too salty.

Sometimes the sea seems to sulk.
It pounds and booms along a beach,
and stings your face with salty spray.
A sulky sea heaves with heavy waves
and makes boats plunge on tossing whitecaps.
A sulky sea is a dull, gloomy sea
that can make you shiver and feel cold.

Sometimes the sea seems angry.
It crashes and smashes over a beach,
and the sound of it buffets your ears.
An angry sea thrashes and churns,
as though something were shaking the world.
An angry sea is a wild sea,
a frightening sea—
a sea you will never forget.

TUMBLING, FLOWING, AND FLOODING

Creeks gurgle,

brooks trickle,

streams gush,

and rivers rush.

If you read through
the next few pages,
you will find that
rocks sometimes flow,

snow sometimes slides,

ground sometimes falls,

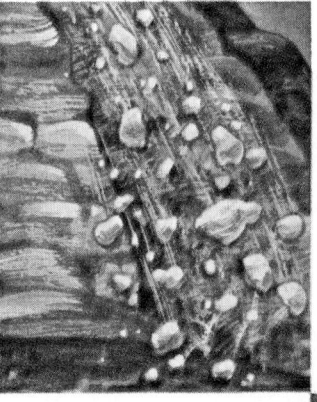

water sometimes
has holes in it,

and that even the sky has a river in it.

WHERE DOES A RIVER BEGIN?

A river can begin
as a tiny trickle of water
gurgling out from under a rock
and flowing down a mountainside.

Showers of raindrops
and rivulets of melted ice or snow
dribble
and plop into the trickle,
and make it bigger
and bigger
until the trickle has become a brook.

Then the brook splashes through a meadow
and into a creek
that burbles past a wood
and into a stream
that tumbles down a hill.

And when brooks,
creeks,
and streams flow together,
they become one river—
a river winding over the land toward the sea.

▲ beginning of the Mississippi

▼ end of the Mississippi

A RIVER TWISTS AND BENDS

A river goes around
anything it cannot wash away.
It winds around boulders,
twists past tangled tree roots,
and bends around hard, rocky ground.

But the twists and bends of a river
are always changing.
As time goes by,
the rushing river water
cuts and carves
new twists and bends.
They loop from side to side,
and meander over the land
like sleepy snakes
slithering slowly across the ground.

OVERFLOWING RIVERS

When rainstorms,
or melting ice and snow,
make a river too big to fit
between its banks, it floods.

Water pours over the banks of the river,
and slowly creeps across the land.
It creeps across fields,
streams over roads,
and swirls around trees.
It can sweep into a town,
covering lawns
and lapping at doorsteps.

But when the rain stops falling,
or the snow stops melting,
the river stops flooding.
And the water creeps slowly back to its bed
between the banks of the river.

WHY DOES
A RIVER ROAR?

Why does a river roar?
You would too,
if you had rocks in your bed.
And when a river flows over rapids,
it has nothing but rocks in its bed.

When a river rushes and tumbles
down a steep slope,
it swoops sand and mud out of its bed
until only rocks are left—
rocks that peep above the surface
of the rushing water.

So the river roars
as it thunders
and pounds,
and sprays,
and crashes over and around,
rushing onward past the rocks
of the river rapids.

WHEN RIVERS FALL DOWN

When a river falls over a rock,
or tumbles and sprays over a cliff,
we say it is a waterfall.
But sometimes a river
makes its own cliff to fall over.
A river's bed is made of rock—
hard rock
and not-so-hard rock, called soft rock.
As a river rushes,
it rubs
and carves,
and wears down the hard rock a little
and the soft rock a lot.

After millions of years,
the soft rock is worn away.
And the river has made a cliff to fall over.
It has made its own waterfall!

Waterfalls are powerful.
The rushing water can turn huge generators
that make enough electricity to light a town.

HOLES IN WATER

No matter how hard you try,
you cannot dig a hole in water.
It justs keeps sloshing around.
The only thing that can make a hole in water
is a whirlpool.
You have probably seen a whirlpool in your bathtub.
When you pull the plug,
the water makes a sucking slurp,
and starts to spin around
as it goes down the drain.

It whirls faster
and faster
until suddenly
there is a hole in the water—
a hole big enough to put your finger in
without getting it wet.

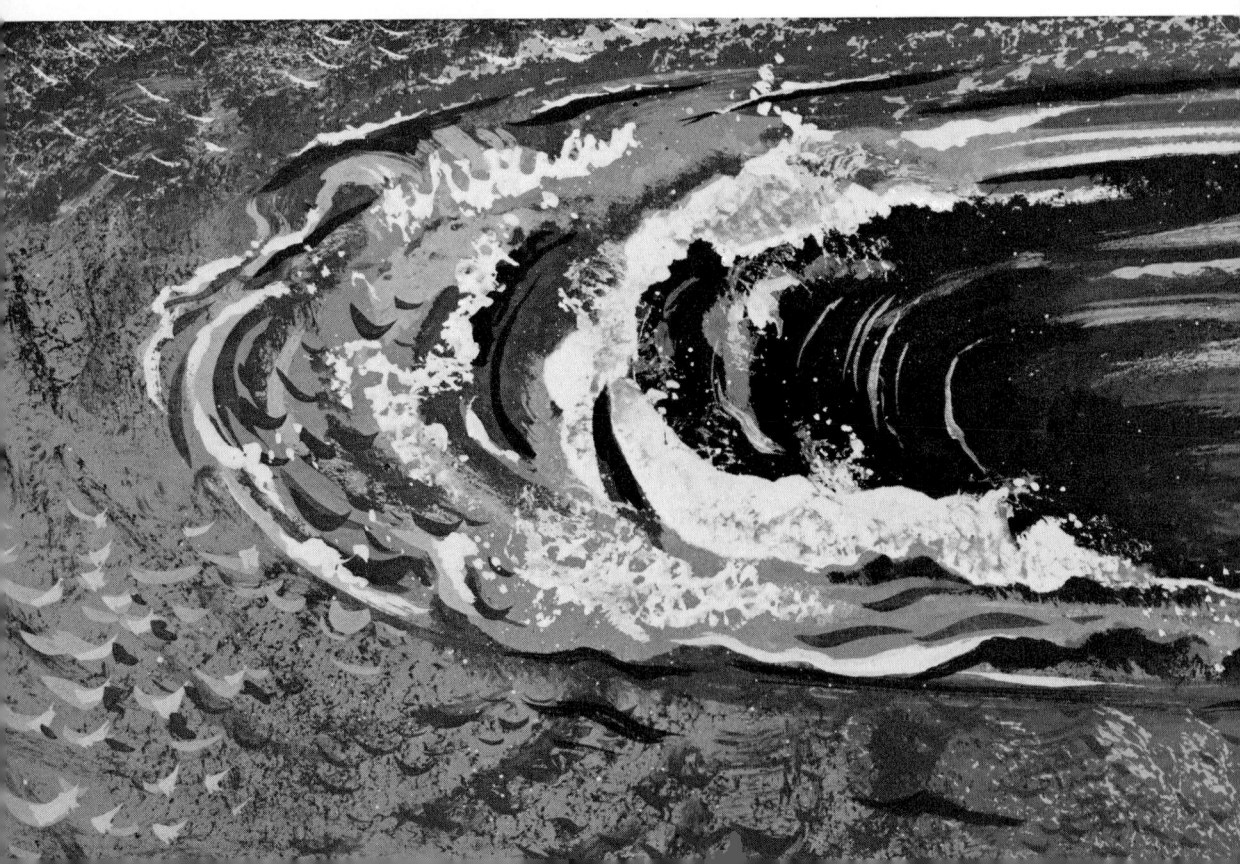

Whirlpools spin in seas, rivers,
and lakes, too.
A rock can make
river water swirl
into a whirlpool,
called an eddy.
And when currents meet
head on in the sea,
they sometimes rush around
as a giant whirlpool,
called a maelstrom.

WHAT STIRS THE SEA?

What stirs the sea?
Wind does!
It blows
and blows.
As it blows across the water,
it stirs part of the sea
into a broad, invisible river.
A river in the middle of the sea
is called a current.

Sometimes the sea even stirs itself.
Where the water is cold, it sinks.
And as it sinks,
currents of warm water rush in to take its place.

Then, too, the earth is spinning all the time.
And as the earth spins,
the ocean water spins.
The spinning of the earth causes each current
to flow in a special direction.

SLIDING SNOW

When snow piles high
on the top of a mountain,
you can start an avalanche just by
clapping your hands
or giving a whistle or shout.

Noise can move snow,
if it is piled in a certain way.
The noise of your clap,
whistle,
or shout shakes the snow.
The snow shifts,
slips,
and starts sliding
and roaring down the mountainside
as an avalanche knocking down everything in its way.

And sometimes,
just the noise of an avalanche booming into a valley
can snap a tree
or knock down a house.

WHEN MOUNTAINS TUMBLE

To crack a log, you need a steel wedge.
But all that is needed to crack a mountain is water.

Drops of water from rain or dew
dribble and seep
into cuts and crevasses in the mountain.
Then, when the sun goes down
and the night gets cold,
the waterdrops freeze.
And as waterdrops freeze, they swell
and split the rock.
All through the night
the ice holds the broken rock together
as though the ice were glue.
But as soon as the sun rises
and warms the air,
the ice melts and the rock falls apart.

Sometimes, the broken bits and chips of rock
start rolling and knocking off
more bits and chips.
Soon thousands of chips, stones,
rocks, and boulders
are tumbling and rumbling down the mountain.
That is one way a landslide starts.

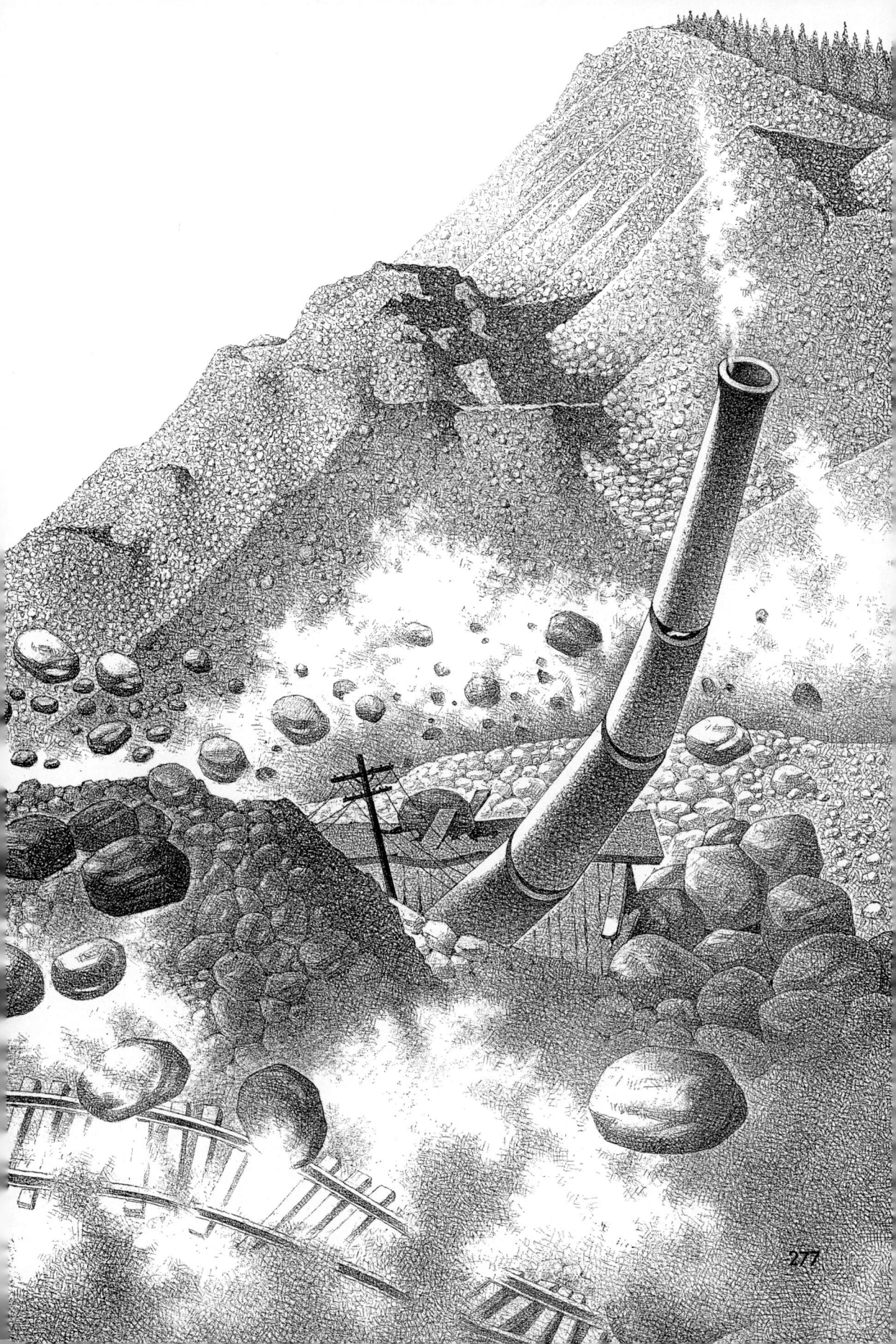

A RIVER

OF ROCK

Imagine a river you could never swim in.
A river that can dazzle you with its glare,
make you choke with its smell,
and prickle your skin with its heat,
even though you are far away.

It is a river of red-hot melted rock
that comes from deep in the earth.
It is called lava.
Lava can bubble and ooze from a hole in the ground
or leak from the side of a volcano.
But even though it is very hot,
lava cools quickly.

And as it cools,
it gets a crust
that cracks
and hardens into giant mud pies,
or towering steeples,
or steps that look like a stairway for giants.

A RIVER OF AIR

High in the sky,
way above the clouds,
there is an invisible river of rushing wind
streaming around the earth.
This river of wind is called the jet stream.

Airplane pilots like to hitch a ride
in the jet stream
when they are going in the same direction.

The jet stream whisks an airplane along so fast,
it can cut the time of a trip in half.
But when a pilot wants to go in the opposite direction,
he keeps away from the jet stream.

If he didn't,
the jet stream would make his airplane
stand still in the air.
It would just be a waste of fuel
to try to fly against this
rushing river of air.

FIRES AND EXPLOSIONS

BOOM can be a thump
on a drum
or the roar
of an exploding volcano.

CRACK can be the snap
of a twig
or the sound of lightning
splitting the air.

WHOOSH can be the noise
of a soaring skyrocket
or the gush of a geyser
squirting into the air.

CRASH can be the clatter
of blocks falling down
or the noise of dust
exploding a barn.

SNAP and CRACKLE
can be the sounds
of logs burning in a fireplace
or the roar of trees
burning in a forest fire.

There are booms
and cracks,
crashes
and crackles,
and snaps that you can read about
on the next few pages.

WHAT IS FIRE?

Fire makes a burning log hiss and pop
with a sudden noise that makes you jump when you're nearly asleep.
Fire can make your face turn pink,
make a marshmallow turn toasty brown,
or make the skin of a chestnut pop.
It can make a dark room flicker
with light from flames in the fireplace.
Or it can be something to stare at
when you wonder about things you will do when you grow up.
But what makes fire?

Fire is a burning gas.
Everything turns into gas
when it gets hot enough.
So when a log gets hot enough,
it starts turning into gas.
And when the heat and the gas mix with air,
they make light—
the light of flames.

Flames to heat with,
flames to see by,
or flames to sit in front of and dream of faraway places.

This Is the Match

This is the match
that burned down a forest.

This is a leaf
that was lit by the match,
that burned down the forest.

This is the twig
that was burned by the leaf,
that was lit by the match,
that burned down the forest.

This is the bush
that was lit by the twig,
that was burned by the leaf,
that was lit by the match,
that burned down the forest.

These were the trees
that were burned by the fire,
that burned the bush,
that was lit by the twig,
that was burned by the leaf,
that was lit by the match,
that burned down the forest.

But who was the person
who could be so careless
as to make the mistake
of dropping the match
that burned down the forest?
Smokey Bear hopes it will never be you.

LIGHTNING FLASHES!

A brilliant streak of lightning zigzags across the sky.
It branches into several forked paths, and
every branch makes a different pattern.
In a flash the whole world seems to light up.

THUNDER ROARS!

What is lightning? What is thunder?
Lightning is a big electric spark.
Sometimes it jumps between a cloud and the ground,
and sometimes between two clouds!
The electric spark is hot.
Its heat splits the air with a tremendous CRACK.
When the spark has passed, the air tumbles together again.
So with each flash of lightning,
you can hear the crack or the rumble of thunder.
Crack! Rumble, rumble, rumble.

How Far Away Is Lightning?

Count the seconds between the flash of light
and the rumble of thunder.
An easy way to count seconds
is to say "THUNDER" after each number.

ONE thunder	——	that's one second.
TWO thunder	——	that's two seconds.
THREE thunder	——	that's three seconds.
FOUR thunder	——	that's four seconds.
FIVE thunder	——	that's five seconds.

It takes about five seconds for sound to travel one mile.
So if you count five seconds, the lightning is a mile away.
If you count ten seconds, the lightning is two miles away.
How far away is it if you count twenty-five seconds?

Most lightning is farther away than you think.
It may be many miles away.
Light travels faster than sound.
You will always see lightning before you hear thunder.
Sometimes you see only the light and don't hear the thunder.
Then the lightning is very far away.

4 thunder

5 thunder

EXPLOSIONS HELP A MOUNTAIN GROW

All rocks are hard.
But some rocks are harder than others.
Hard rock and not-so-hard rock lie
beneath the earth like a wiggly layer cake—
one layer on top of the other.

Heat and explosions deep inside the earth
heave, move, and wrinkle the layers of rock.
Rock is pushed,
squeezed,
and tilted in layers.
The layers bend,
stretch,
drop,
and rise.
Slowly a mountain
pokes its peak
above the ground.

Most mountains grow so slowly
that they hardly seem to change
at all.
Only after millions and millions of years,
a mountain becomes
big and tall.

A MOUNTAIN WITH

A HOLE IN THE MIDDLE

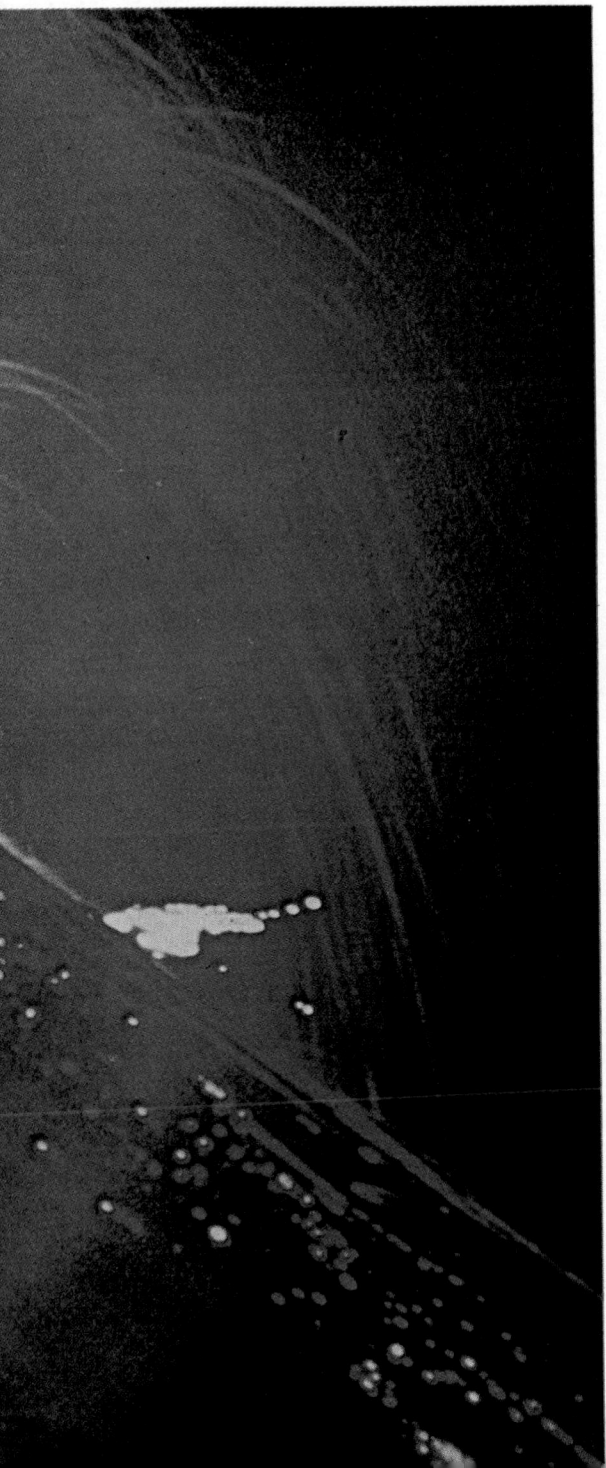

The earth trembles
and shakes,
rumbles
and splits,
and black smoke pours out
of a hole in the ground.

BOOM!
The earth explodes.
Smoke
and ash
and cinders
spit and spew
high into the air.

Deep under the earth it is so hot
that the rock melts
into a red-hot gooey liquid.
The melted rock, called lava,
flows out of the crack in the ground.
It oozes over the ground.
Then it cools and hardens into rock.
More and more lava
piles up and hardens.
A mountain has begun to rise—
a mountain called a volcano.

WHY DO

When geysers gush,
some squirt water so high
that it seems to disappear in the sky.
Others hardly squirt water high enough
to hit a mouse in the eye.
But why do geysers gush at all?

The main part of a geyser
is a deep hole in the ground
that is like a tube and is full of water.
Hot rocks heat the water at the bottom of the tube.
The water gets hotter and hotter,
and the pressure greater and greater,
until suddenly, WHOOSH!

GEYSERS GUSH?

The water at the bottom of the tube
explodes into steam.
The steam pushes against
the water above it
and rams it up the tube.

Then, with a deep, rumbling gurgle,
the water shoots straight up into the air,
then spreads
in a shower of waterdrops
that spatter back to the ground.

How Wind Explodes a House

There is a kind of wind that can make a house explode.
Not a whispering kind of wind that tugs a kite into the sky,
or a puffing kind of wind that billows your shirt,
but a howling, whirling kind of wind called a tornado.

With a noise like the roar of a thousand lions,
a tornado screams over a house.
Swoosh!
Suddenly, all the air around the house
is gone—
sucked away by the whirling wind.
Boom! Air inside the house
bursts out,
and the house explodes like a balloon.
The explosion pops out windows,
blows down walls,
and tears off the roof.
Shattered glass
and splinters of walls and roof
whirl away in the wind.

But if windows and doors of a house
are open when a tornado strikes,
the air can rush out the windows,
and swirl out the doorways,
without blowing the house to pieces.

297

WATER FROM AN EXPLOSION

Water is formed
when two gases come together—
a gas called hydrogen
and a gas called oxygen.
And it takes an explosion
to turn the two gases into water.

The heat of a fiery volcano,
or a lightning bolt,
or even the flame of a match
can make hydrogen,
and oxygen
mingle
and explode with a bang.

And after the bang,
there is water—
water that can put out the hot flame of a match.

WHAT BLEW

Crash!
Suddenly, a barn collapses
and tumbles to the ground.
Did an earthquake shake it down?
Did a wind blow it over?
Did a horse kick it down?
Did an angry bull butt it over?
Did a rotting beam give way?
Was the hay in the loft too heavy to hold?
No, these weren't the reasons.

THE BARN DOWN?

Dust knocked down the barn—
hay-dust that exploded
and blew it down.
The dust exploded because
a mouse, on its way out of the barn,
stopped to chew on a wire.
The wire was an electric wire
that spat a spark
and lit the dust,
which burned so fast it exploded
and blew down the barn.

WHEN THERE SEEMS TO BE NO REASON

Sometimes a fire starts
when there seems to be no reason.
No one started it with a match.
No one dropped a burning cigarette.
No one left the stove burner on.
Still, the fire started!

There really is a reason for the fire.
It didn't start by magic.
Something got hot—
hot enough to cause a fire to start.

The fire can start in many ways—
sometimes by chemicals being too close together,
sometimes by the sun overheating a closed place,
and sometimes even by tiny animals, called bacteria!
Most people call this kind of fire SPONTANEOUS COMBUSTION.
But scientists call it SPONTANEOUS IGNITION.

Here's how a spontaneous combustion fire might start.
Bacteria live in haystacks
and eat away at the hay.
And as they eat,
their bodies heat the hay.
The more they eat,
the hotter the hay becomes.
The hay gets hotter,
and hotter,
and hotter
until suddenly, *poof!*
Some tiny bits of hay start to burn.
Soon the whole haystack
is a roaring fire—
a spontaneous combustion fire!

These are some fires that can start
by spontaneous combustion.

ROUND, SQUARE,

You know that
a ball is a ball
because it is round.

You know that
a block is a block
because it has
many flat sides
and sharp corners.

You know that
an ice-cream cone
is an ice-cream cone
because of its shape.

AND BUMPY

You even know
which Teddy bear is yours
because of its shape.

But did you also know that

salt,

and raindrops,

and snowflakes,
and icicles
all have special shapes, too?
On the next few pages
you will find out
about the special shapes
that many things have.

The Shape of the Earth

You have heard that the earth is round.
But how could you prove it to someone?

If you live near the sea
or a big lake,
you could tell him to watch the ships
as they sail toward the skyline.
The ships get
smaller
and smaller
as they sail farther and farther away.

But when the ships reach the skyline,
the bottoms seem to disappear
and only the tops of them can be seen.
Then, even the tops seem to disappear
as they sail on around the earth.

If you are riding in a car
toward some mountains,
you can see the peaks of the mountains
long before you see the entire mountains.
The roundness of the earth
hides the bottom of the mountains
from view.

And pictures of the earth taken
by astronauts
show the roundness of the earth.

ROCKS THAT GROW INTO SHAPES

Animals grow.
Plants grow.
But did you know
that some rocks grow, too?
Rocks that grow are called crystals.
If the crystals are in a liquid,
they can grow from tiny specks into large stones.
And as each kind of crystal grows,
it keeps its own special shape.

As gold,
salt,
and silver crystals grow,
they keep the shape of cubes.

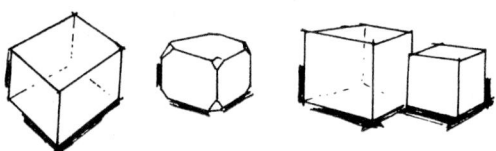

Salt crystals that have grown together

As topaz,
barite,
and sulfur crystals grow,
they keep the shape of long blocks.

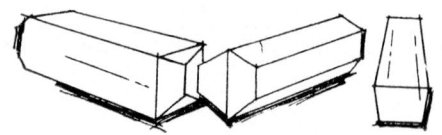

A broken piece of a sulfur crystal

As alum,
pyrite,
and garnet crystals grow,
they keep the shape
of two pyramids stuck together.

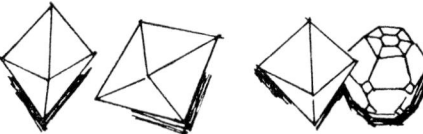

Iron pyrite crystals stuck together in a rock

A broken beryl crystal stuck in rock

As corundum,
beryl,
and cinnabar crystals grow,
they keep the shape of long triangles
that look like prisms.

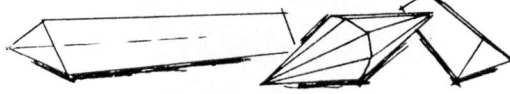

As quartz,
borax,
gypsum,
and arsenic crystals grow,
they keep a shape
something like a diamond.

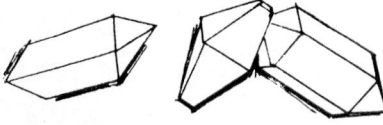

A broken quartz crystal

Staurolite crystals with tiny garnets in them

As turquoise
and staurolite crystals grow,
they keep odd shapes
that look like roses or crosses.

HOW TO GROW

You can grow big crystals of your own
with tiny crystals of table salt.

Put some hot water into a small piepan.
Then put a few spoonfuls of salt
into the water and stir it until it dissolves.
Now put the pan in a place
where it will not be disturbed for a few days.
When all the water is gone,
you will have square salt crystals.

YOUR OWN CRYSTALS

You can also grow
alum,
Rochelle salt,
and sodium chlorate crystals
in Mason jars.
You can get these things at your drugstore.
Dissolve the alum, or Rochelle salt,
or sodium chlorate in water.
Hang a string in the jar,
and the crystals will grow on the string.

312

STONE STRAWS
AND
STONE CURTAINS

Where can you find
parachutes made of stone,
or stone soda straws,
or stone in the shape
of an atomic cloud,
or ribbons made of stone,
or stone that looks like lace,
or stone curtains
that look like bacon strips?

You can find them
deep inside a cave.
Water drips and drips
and carries tiny bits of rock
that pile up
into rocklike plates.
Water cuts and carves
fantastic and bizarre
shapes in the stone.

ROCK

I see a mushroom.
But it is not a mushroom
that I can eat.
It is really just a rock
that looks like a mushroom.

Stone Mountain, Georgia

I see a monstrous tree trunk.
But it is not a tree trunk
that I can chop.
It is really just a rock
that looks like a tree trunk.

Devils Tower, Wyoming

I see a castle.
But it is not a castle
that I can play in.
It is really just a cluster of rocks
that looks like a castle.

Bryce Canyon, Utah

PICTURES

I see some skyscrapers.
But they are not really skyscrapers!
They are really just cliffs
that look like skyscrapers.

El Morro, New Mexico

I see a needle.
But it is not a needle
that I can sew with.
It is really just a rock
that looks like a needle.

The Needles, South Dakota

I see a man's face.
But it is not a face
that feels soft when I touch it.
It is really just a rock
that looks like a man's face.

Wind and rain carved them all.

Profile Mountain, New Hampshire

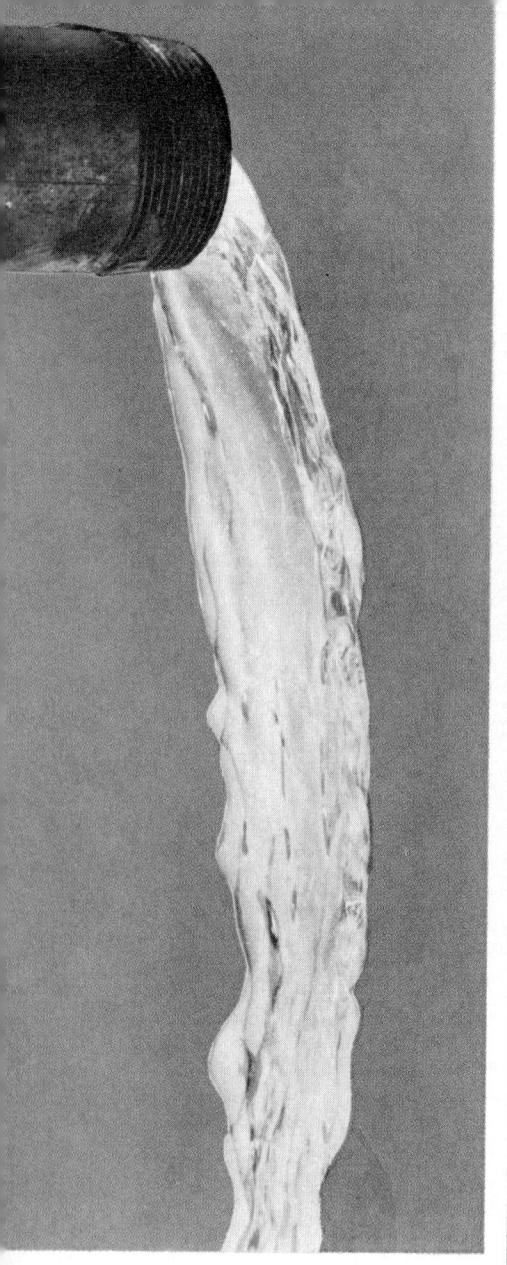

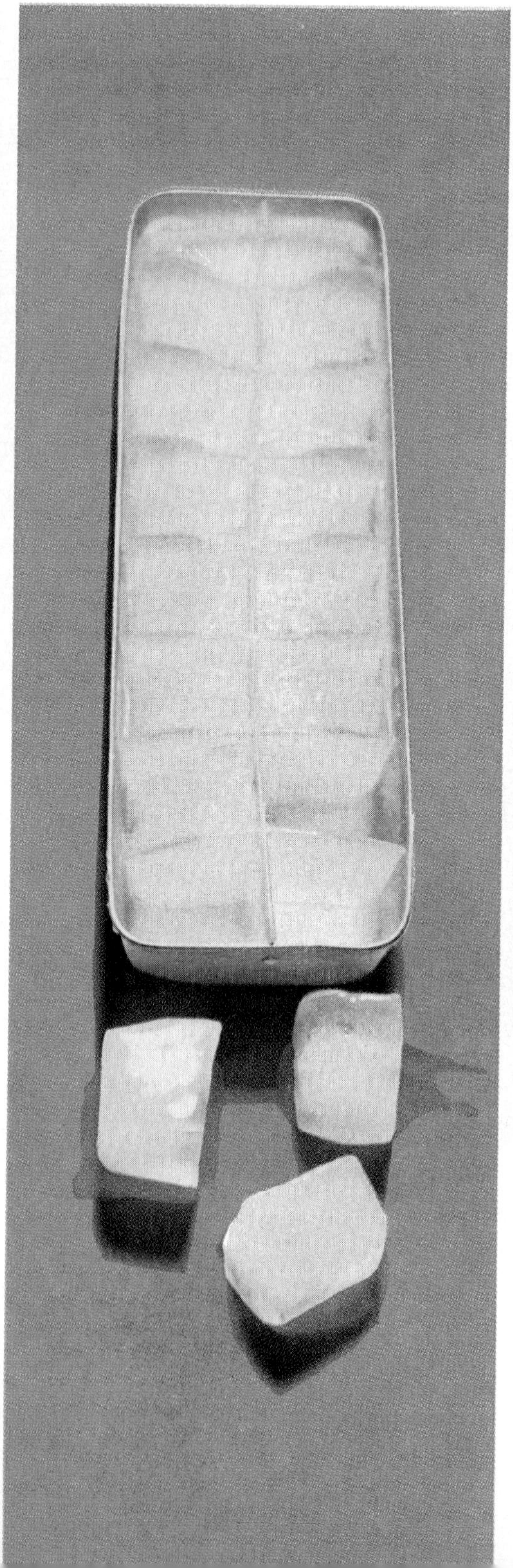

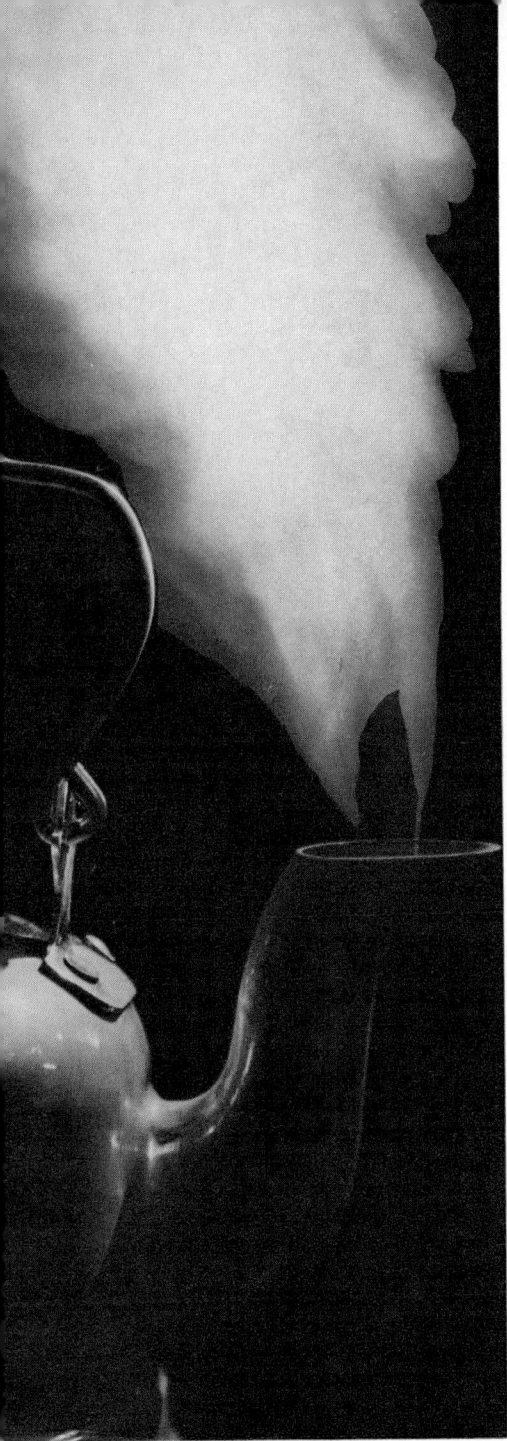

WHAT
WATER
CAN BE

You can find water
that is wet and runny
like the water you wash your hands with.
Then water is a *liquid*.

You can find water
that is hard and cold
like the ice you put in your cold drinks.
Then water is a *solid*.

And there is even water
all around you that you can't see.

If you put water into a pan
over a hot stove,
it will turn into water vapor.
And water vapor is a *gas*.

Water is not the only thing
that can be a solid, a liquid, or a gas.
Every thing can become
a solid, a liquid or a gas
if you heat it
or cool it enough—
cereal can, crackers can, and cookies can.
So can doorknobs, coat hangers,
and bicycle handle bars,
or shoes, shirts, and book covers,
or even rocks.

OXBOW LAKES

Lakes can have many shapes.
Some are long and skinny.
Some look like circles.
Some look like wiggly snakes.
And some are shaped like crescents.
How do they get these different shapes?

Most lakes just happen to be
the shape of the dents in the earth that they fill.
But a lake that is shaped like a crescent
is made by a river.
It is called an oxbow lake.

A river goes around anything it can't go through.
The bends of a river sometimes make
a loop.
As the river flows, it carries
rocks,
dirt,
and silt.
Sometimes the river piles the dirt
and rocks
at a narrow part
of the loop.

The rocks, dirt, and silt
are piled so high that soon
the loop of water
is completely cut off
from the main part of the river.
The part of the loop of water that is left
looks like a crescent.
And this is an oxbow lake.

ICY DAGGERS

When I look out my window
on a cold and blustery day,
I can see icy daggers
hanging in front of me.

They are the icicles made
when snow melts on my roof
and starts to trickle as water
slowly to the ground.
But the air is so cold
that the water freezes
before it can drip from the roof—
it freezes into an icicle.

Icicles can be
short and skinny,
or long and fat,
depending upon how much
and how fast the water drips.
They can hang down a little way
or hang all the way down to the ground.

322

THE SHAPES THAT FALL FROM THE SKY

All raindrops are round
until they hit the ground.
Then they can splatter
into special shapes
like umbrellas,
or kings' crowns.

All snowflakes have six points
when you look at them under a magnifying glass.
But no one has ever found
two snowflakes
that look the same.

Snow pellets have many different shapes.
Some are small and round.
And some are small and bumpy.

Bits of ice that glitter like diamonds are called ice prisms.
Some are shaped like needles.
And some are shaped like bullets.

The sleet that rat-a-tat-tats on your rooftop
is made of ice pellets.
The pellets are shaped like round beads
and bounce like little marbles on anything they hit.

Hailstones
are round
and sometimes lopsided.
They are bumpy stones
that can be as big as baseballs.

The Shape of My Shadow

What is long and skinny in the morning,
short and squat at noon,
and long and skinny again in the afternoon?
MY SHADOW!
As long as the sun is shining,
wherever I go
my shadow goes with me.

As I move,
my shadow moves, too.
Sometimes it is at my side,
and sometimes it is in front of me,
and sometimes it is behind me.

No matter how hard I try,
I cannot run away from my shadow
or catch my shadow
until the sun stops shining.
Then I have no shadow at all.

WHAT IS IT?

These are all close-up pictures of things you have probably seen.

Can you guess what they are?

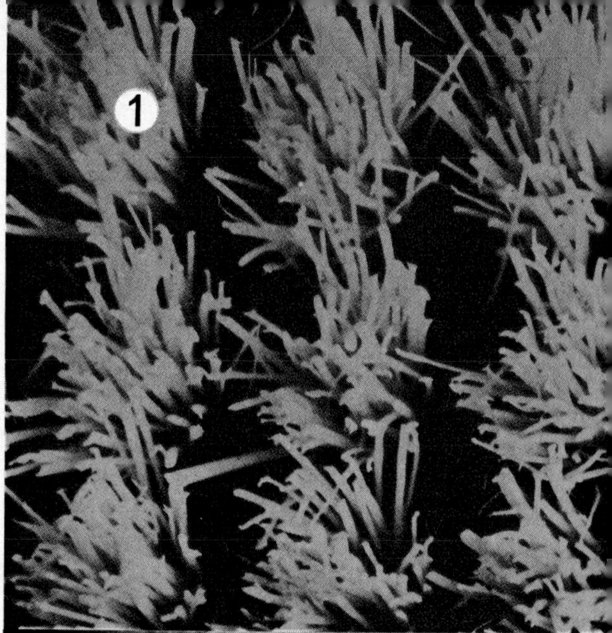

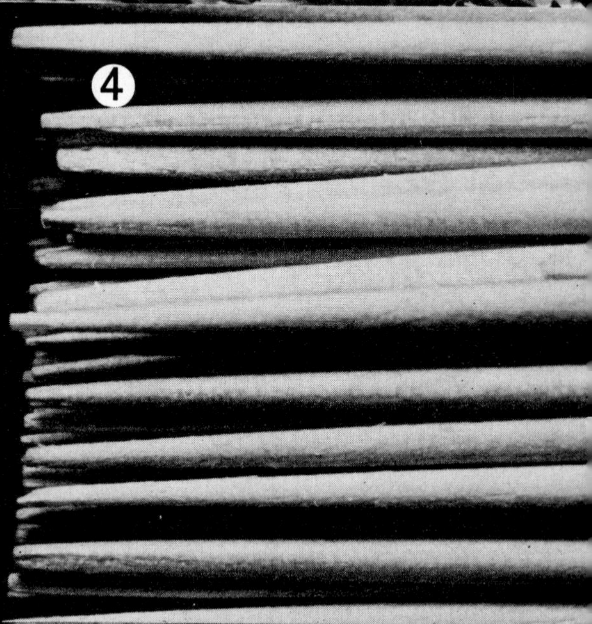

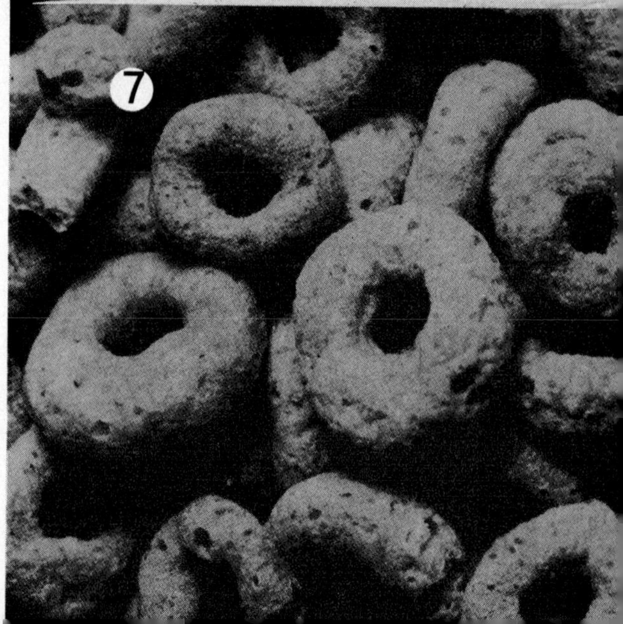

AGAIN AND AGAIN

You will always have

night and day,

sunrise

and sunset,

summer

and winter,

spring

and fall,

full moons 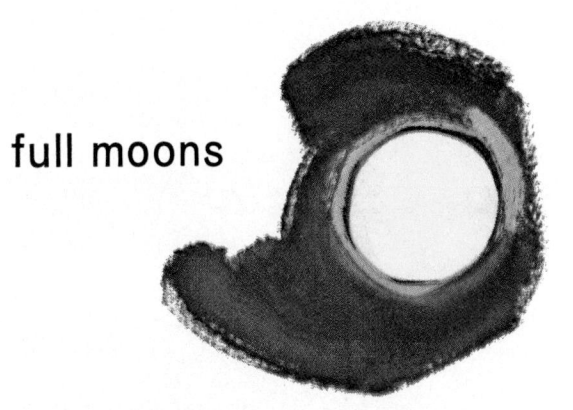 and new moons,

high tides  and low tides,

and waves that heave up and down.

These things never stop happening.
They will go on and on,
again and again,
and
again
and
again.

NIGHT AND DAY

When you get up in the morning,
a child on the other side of the world
is going to bed.
And he does not get up
until it is time
for you to go to bed.

When it is daytime where you live,
it is nighttime on the other side of the world.

And when it is nighttime where you live,
it is daytime on the other side of the world.

It is always daytime for the part of the world
that faces the sun.

But the world is always spinning.
The part of the world that faces the sun
soon spins away from the sun,
and it becomes nighttime
for that part of the world.

SUNRISE AND SUNSET

In the morning when the sky is
black,
then gray,
then red,
then orange,
then pink,
then blue,
we say that the sun is rising.
And we call it a sunrise.

And at night when the sky is
blue,
then pink,
then orange,
then red,
then gray,
then black,
we say that the sun is setting.
And we call it a sunset.

But the sun really does not
rise
or set.
It does not move across our sky at all.
The earth spins around to make night and day.
And in the morning we see the sun.
But at night it disappears.

The day can be dark and dreary when clouds hide the sun,
or it can be bright and sunny when there are no clouds.
But there is always
a sunrise and a sunset, even though
you may not be able to see it.

THE
FOUR
SEASONS

Spring is the time of year when
the leaves and grass begin to grow,
flowers start to bud,
birds sing and twitter,
and the weather gets warm and balmy.

Summer is the time of year when
lots of flowers are in bloom,
cicadas drone,
bees buzz,
mosquitoes bite,
and the weather gets hot.

Fall is the time of year when
the leaves turn orange, red, or yellow,
squirrels hide their nuts,
farmers harvest their crops,
and the weather gets cool.

Winter is the time of year when
there are no leaves on the trees,
snow may cover the ground,
bears, woodchucks, and dormice hibernate,
and the weather gets cold.

Summer always follows spring.
Fall always follows summer.
Winter always follows fall.
And spring always follows winter,
year after year, over and over again.

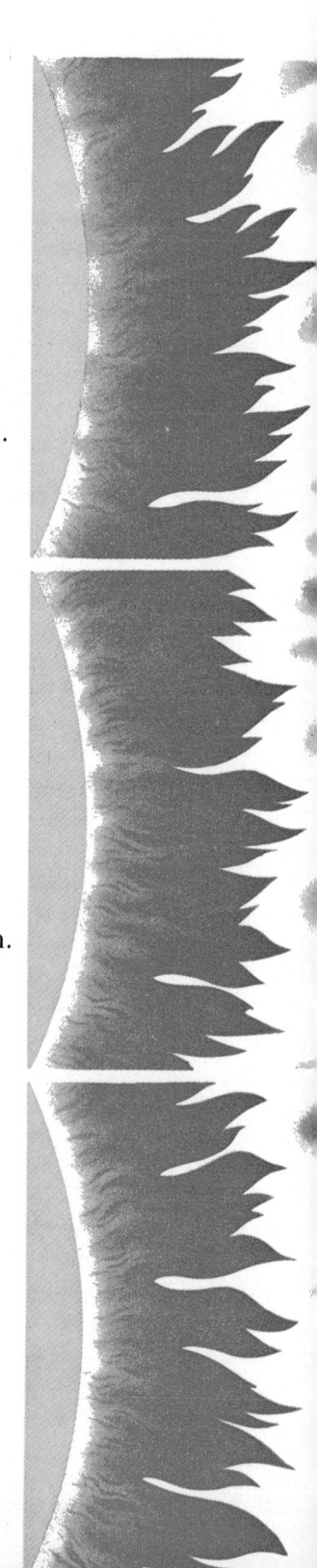

We have seasons
because the earth is tipped
as it whirls around the sun.
Sometimes the North Pole
points in the direction of the sun,
and sometimes it points away from the sun.

When the North Pole is pointed toward the sun,
the weather gets hot for people who live
in the northern half of the world—it's summer for them.
And the weather gets cold for people who live
in the southern half of the world—it's winter for them.

When the North Pole is pointed away from the sun,
the weather gets cold for people who live
in the northern half of the world—it's winter for them.
And the weather gets hot for people who live
in the southern half of the world—it's summer for them.

Sometimes the North Pole is neither pointed
away from the sun nor pointed toward the sun.
It is in between.
And the weather is in between, too.
Sometimes it is warm.
Sometimes it is cool.
Then it's spring or fall.

THE EVER-CHANGING MOON

Sometimes when you look
at the moon,
you see
a big white ball.
Sometimes you see
half a ball.
Sometimes you see
just a moon slice.
And sometimes you see
hardly any moon at all.

You would never see the moon
if there were no sun.
The moon has no light of its own.
So you only see it
because the sun shines on it.

When you can see the whole face of the moon,
it is called a full moon.
After one week, the full moon looks like a half-moon.
After one more week, the half-moon
looks like hardly any moon at all.
Then it is called a new moon.
After one more week, the new moon
looks like a half-moon again.
And after one more week, the half-moon
looks like a full moon again.

The moon is an earth satellite,
and it whirls around the earth.
Sometimes the moon is in that part of the sky
where we see sunshine on its whole face.
Then we have a full moon.
But at other times the moon is in that part of the sky
where we see sunshine on only part of its face.

WHERE DID THE MOON GO?

At certain times of the year
the moon disappears from the sky.
Suddenly, part of the big white ball is gone,
and then after a little while
there is no moon at all.
In a short time a little part of the moon begins to show.
And then more and more shows
until it is a big white ball again.

Where did the moon go?
The moon was hidden by the earth.
The earth and the moon
are both lighted by the sun.
When the earth spins
between the sun and the moon,
it blots out the sun's light and
the earth hides the moon for a little while.
But soon the moon spins out of the earth's shadow
and the sun can light it again.

When we see the moon disappear this way,
we say we have seen an eclipse of the moon.

Pictures of the moon taken from the same place
at different times during an eclipse.

WHEN THE SUN DISAPPEARS

Sometimes when the sun is shining
like a ball of fire in the sky,
a little chunk of the sun suddenly
seems to disappear.
And then more and more of it disappears
until there is only a black dot
with a circle of light around it.
After a little while, a bit of the sun shows.
Then more and more of it appears
until it is like a ball of fire in the sky again.

The sun will disappear this way when the moon
spins between the earth and the sun.
Then it hides the sun from the earth for a little while.
When we see the sun disappear this way,
we say we have seen an eclipse of the sun.

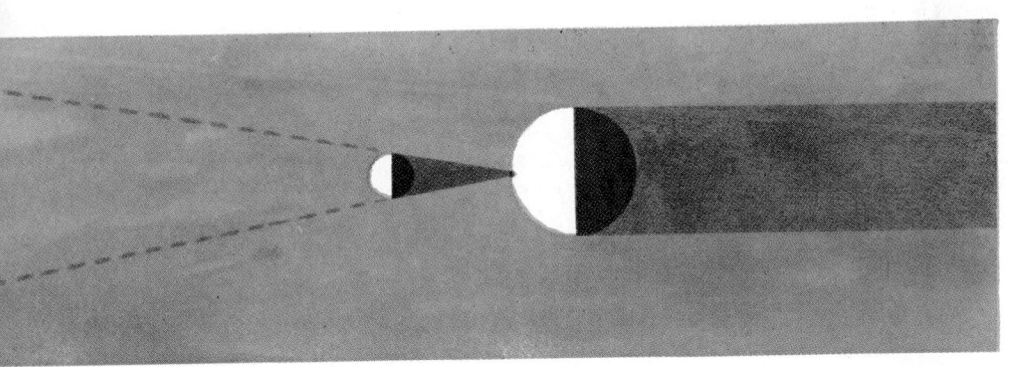

Pictures of the sun taken from the same place
at different times during an eclipse.

DO WAVES MAKE WATER MOVE?

The middle of the ocean heaves
up and down,
up and down,
Splish! Splash! Sploosh!

It may look as if the ocean water is moving
forward and backward,
but it's not!

344

It just goes
up and down like
a bouncing ball,
or a teeter-totter,
or an old butter churn,
or an oil-well drill,
or a water pump,
or a yo-yo,
as the white-capped peaks of water seem to pass by.

If you want to be sure of this,
throw a piece of cork
into wavy water
and watch it bob
up and down,
over and over again.

You will see that it stays
right where you threw it,
bouncing up and down,
but not moving
forward or backward.

THE OCEAN

If you lived near the ocean,
you would not need a clock
to tell you the time of day.

You could tell time by the tides.
Tides are the rise and fall of the ocean waters.
And they occur only at certain times during the day.

CLOCK

When the water is at high tide, it covers the beach.
And when it is at low tide, the beach shows.

It is the pull of the moon that causes tides.

The moon pulls on the waters of the earth
the way a magnet pulls on a piece of steel.

Illustration
Acknowledgments

The publishers of CHILDCRAFT gratefully acknowledge the courtesy of the following artists, photographers, publishers, agencies, and corporations for illustrations in the volume. Page numbers refer to two-page spreads. The words "(left)," "(center)," "(top)," "(bottom)," and "(right)," indicate position on the spread. All illustrations are the exclusive property of the publishers of CHILDCRAFT unless names are marked with an asterisk (°).

4–5: Jim Weathers
6–7: Richard Loehle—Grant-Jacoby, Inc.
8–9: (left) Helmut Wimmer from *Natural History* Magazine (°); (right) Richard Loehle—Grant-Jacoby, Inc.
10–11: photo by Rie Gaddis; art by Suzi Hawes
12–13: art by Jill Lillard; photos, (left) Ewing Galloway (°), (right) U.S. Weather Bureau (°), Samuel Myslis (°)
14–15: U.S. Air Force (°)
16–17: (left) Ronny Jacques, Photo Researchers (°); (right) Richard Loehle—Grant-Jacoby, Inc.
18–19: Alex Ebel
20–21: (left) Alex Ebel; (right) Lick Observatory (°)
22–23: photo, © California Institute of Technology (°); art by Richard Loehle—Grant-Jacoby, Inc.
24–25: Jim Weathers
26–27: (left) Jim Weathers; (right) Chicago Natural History Museum (°)
28–29: Three Lions (°)
30–31: Neal Cochran
32–33: Don Almquist
34–35: Jill Lillard
36–37: (left) Don Almquist; (right) Ray Atkenson (°)
38–39: art by Don Almquist; photo by Barbara Morgan (°)
40–41: Bob and Ira Spring (°)
42–43: photo, U.S. Weather Bureau (°); art by Neal Cochran
44–45: James H. Brown
46–47: U.S. Weather Bureau (°)
48–49: photo by Ray Atkenson (°); art by Suzi Hawes
50–51: John M. Bolt, Jr.
52–53: (top and center) Ray Atkenson (°), (bottom) Air Preheater Corp. (°)
54–55: Jill Lillard
56–57: Raymond Perlman
58–59: John M. Bolt, Jr.
60–61: (left) Air Pollution Control District, City of Los Angeles (°); (right) Milo Williams (°)

62–63: James H. Brown
64–65: Raymond Perlman
66–67: photo, Luoma Photos (°); art by Don Taka
68–69: (left) U.S. Weather Bureau (°); (right) Mendelsohn, Black Star (°)
70–71: Tom Gorman—Stevens-Gross Studios, Inc.
72–73: Roswell Brown
74–75: Jill Lillard
76–77: Morris Rosenfeld, courtesy ANSCO (°)
78–79: Richard Loehle—Grant-Jacoby, Inc.
80–81: Jill Lillard
82–83: Raymond Perlman
84–85: photo by Frank Cassidy (°); art by Richard Loehle—Grant-Jacoby, Inc.
86–87: Wide World (°)
88–89: United Press Int. (°)
90–91: photos, U.S. Navy (°); art by John M. Bolt, Jr.
92–93: (left) U.S. Weather Bureau (°); (right) Brian Brake, Magnum (°)
94–95: Library of Congress (°)
96–97: Neal Cochran
98–99: © California Institute of Technology (°)
100–101: Neal Cochran
102–103: Clifford Birklund
104–105: (left) U.S. Navy (°); (right) photo, National Film Board of Canada (°), art by Neal Cochran
106–107: art by Neal Cochran; photo, Mt. Wilson and Palomar Observatories (°)
108–109: art by Neal Cochran; photo, mural by Chesley Bonestell—courtesy of the Museum of Science, Boston (°)
110–111: Neal Cochran
112–113: Alex Ebel
114–115: Alex Ebel
116–117: Alex Ebel
118–119: art by Neal Cochran; photo, American Telephone and Telegraph Co. (°)
120–121: Neal Cochran
122–123: art by Neal Cochran; photo, Mt. Wilson and Palomar Observatories (°)

124–125: Neal Cochran
126–127: Neal Cochran
128–129: Raymond Perlman
130–131: Robert Kresin
132–133: (*left*) Dick Meek for *Sports Illustrated* (°); (*right*) Dr. Hugo Benioff (°)
134–135: Don Stebbing
136–137: W. Imber from Conzett & Huber (°)
138–139: Ned Haines, Rapho-Guillumette (°)
140–141: Carl Yates
142–143: art by Neal Cochran; photo by H. G. Ponting from Paul Popper (°)
144–145: (*left*) Neal Cochran; (*right*) photo, Southern Pacific Lines (°), sculpture by Suzi Hawes
146–147: Raymond Perlman
148–149: photography by Mary and Loren Root, FPSA; art by Bill Hammond
150–151: photography by Mary and Loren Root, FPSA; art by Robert Kresin
152–153: photo, U.S. Bureau of Mines (°); art by Bill Hammond
154–155: Mary and Loren Root, FPSA
156–157: art by Vernon McKissack; photos, (*left*) Louisiana Department of Commerce and Industry (°), (*right*) U.S. Borax & Chemical Corp. (°)
158–159: art by Robert Kresin; photography by Mary and Loren Root, FPSA
160–161: (*left*) Josef Muench (°); (*right*) Mary and Loren Root, FPSA
162–163: Vernon McKissack
164–165: (*left*) Ray Atkenson (°); (*right*) James T. Mitchell (°)
166–167: Erick Heinigen, Rapho-Guillumette (°)
168–169: Carl Yates
170–171: U.S. Geological Survey (°)
172–173: Raymond Perlman
174–175: *California Highways and Public Works* (°)
176–177: (*top*) Fairchild Aerial Surveys, Inc. (°); (*bottom*) Utah Tourist and Publicity Council (°)
178–179: H. Armstrong Roberts (°)
180–181: art by Raymond Perlman; photo, Ewing Galloway (°)
182–183: Josef Muench (°)
184–185: Josef Muench (°)
186–187: H. Armstrong Roberts (°)
188–189: Josef Muench (°)
190–191: photo by Emil Schulthess, Black Star (°); art by Neal Cochran
192–193: (*left*) National Park Service (°), Union Pacific Railroad (°); (*right*) Ewing Galloway (°), Union Pacific Railroad (°), Utah Tourist and Publicity Council (°)
194–195: Raymond Perlman
196–197: (*left*) Bill Shrout, reprinted by permission of *The Saturday Evening Post* © 1961 Curtis Publishing Co. (°); (*right*) Commonwealth of Virginia Department of Conservation and Economic Development (°)
198–199: Josef Muench (°)
200–201: Bradford Washburn (°)
202–203: Bradley Smith, Rapho-Guillumette (°)
204–205: Bob and Ira Spring
206–207: Joseph Cellini
208–209: Neal Cochran
210–211: photo courtesy Armstrong Cork Co. (°); art by Bill Hammond
212–213: (*left*) Don Stebbing; (*right*) photo, Chicago Aerial Survey (°), art by Bill Hammond
214–215: (*left*) City of Chicago (°); (*right*) Chicago Aerial Survey (°), Don Stebbing
216–217: map adaptation courtesy © Rand McNally & Co. (°); art by Neal Cochran
218–219: Neal Cochran
220–221: Shirley Krimsin
222–223: photo by Don Stebbing; art by Shirley Krimsin
224–225: Don Loehle
226–227: Joseph Watson Little
228–229: (*left*) Don Stebbing; (*right*) U.S. Coast and Geodetic Survey (°)
230–231: Vernon McKissack
232–233: Don Stebbing
234–235: U.S. Coast and Geodetic Survey (°)
236–237: Neal Cochran
238–239: Don Stebbing
240–241: (*left*) Robert Goodman, Black Star © National Geographic Society (°); (*right*) U.S. Coast and Geodetic Survey (°)
242–243: John Henry—Stephens Biondi De Cicco Inc.
244–245: photo, U.S. Navy (°); art by Bill Hammond
246–247: photo by Arthur Griffin (°); art by Joseph Watson Little
248–249: (*left*) photo by Erika Stone, P.I.P. (°); (*right*) Alex Ebel
250–251: (*left*) Christian Vibe (°); (*right*) Don Stebbing
252–253: Gurney Miller
254–255: art by Joseph Watson Little; photo by Robert C. Hermes, National Audubon Society (°)
256–257: (*top*) L. A. Ketring, Shostal (°); (*center*) Shelly Grossman, Shostal (°); (*bottom*) H. Lambert, Shostal (°)
258–259: Raymond Perlman
260–261: (*top*) Tom Hollyman, Photo Researchers (°); (*bottom*) Fritz Henle, Photo Researchers (°)
262–263: (*left*) Phillip V. Inskipp-Hawkins; (*right*) courtesy *Life* Magazine © Time, Inc. (°)
264–265: photo, United Press Int. (°); art by Bill Hammond
266–267: (*left*) Josef Muench (°); (*right*) Malak, Three Lions (°)
268–269: (*left*) CHILDCRAFT photo; (*right*) Harrison Forman, Publix Pictorial (°)
270–271: art by Mary Hauge; photo by Don Stebbing
272–273: Humble Oil and Refining Company (°)
274–275: Rudolf Freund
276–277: Rudolf Freund
278–279: (*left*) Wide World (°); (*right*) J. Allan Cash (°)
280–281: Alex Ebel
282–283: Raymond Perlman
284–285: John Henry—Stephens Biondi De Cicco Inc.
286–287: (*left*) Raymond Perlman; (*right*) U.S. Department of Agriculture, Forest Service—courtesy of the Advertising Council and Association of State Foresters (°)
288–289: photo, Monkmeyer (°); art by Neal Cochran
290–291: Bradford Washburn (°)
292–293: John Walters (°)
294–295: Ray Manley, Shostal (°)
296–297: Gurney Miller
298–299: Robert Addison—Stevens-Gross Studios, Inc.
300–301: Neal Cochran
302–303: Roy Andersen
304–305: Jill Lillard
306–307: John Henry—Stephens Biondi De Cicco Inc.
308–309: (*left and top three right*) Don Stebbing; (*bottom right*) Mary and Loren Root, FPSA
310–311: Don Stebbing
312–313: (*left*) Commonwealth of Virginia Department of Conservation Economic Development (°); (*right*) Gerald R. Massie, Missouri Division of Resources and Development (°)
314–315: all photos by Josef Muench (°) except: (*top left*) Stone Mountain Memorial Association (°), (*bottom right*) Shostal (°)
316–317: (*left to right*) James H. Brown, Don Stebbing, Ewing Galloway (°)
318–319: U.S. Department of Agriculture (°)
320–321: photo by Clemens Kalischer (°); art by Bill Hammond
322–323: (*left*) Ewing Galloway (°); (*right*) James H. Brown
324–325: Don Stebbing
326–327: Don Stebbing
328–329: Jim Weathers
330–331: (*left*) Don Loehle; (*right*) Neal Cochran
332–333: (*left*) Russ Kinne, Photo Researchers (°); (*right*) Arthur Griffin (°)
334–335: Leo Skidmore—courtesy Stephens Biondi De Cicco Inc. (°)
336–337: Alex Ebel
338–339: (*left*) Yerkes Observatory (°); (*right*) Kaufmann & Fabry (°)
340–341: photo, *The Minneapolis Star* (°); art by Raymond Perlman
342–343: photo adapted from United Press Int. (°); art by Raymond Perlman
344–345: Tom Gorman—Stevens-Gross Studios, Inc.
346–347: Arthur Griffin (°)

Index to Volume 3

Each entry in this index is listed under both its general and its specific name. For example, weather can be found under the general term "weather" and under the specific terms "rain," "snow," "sleet," "hail."

Additional material on the world in space can be found in other volumes by consulting the general CHILDCRAFT index in Volume 15.

Agate, 155
Air, 56–59, 67, 68, 82, 83, 87
Air current, 22, 76, 78, 79, 280, 281
Air pressure, 31, 90, 297
Alum crystal, 309, 311
Amethyst, 159
Animals, weather forecasting, 54, 55
Arsenic crystal, 309
Arsenopyrite, 157
Artesian well, 180
Artificial satellite, 118
Asbestos, 155
Ash, 49, 64, 185
Asteroid, 125
Astronaut, 22, 96, 97, 106, 111, 115
Astronomy, 20–25, 96–127
Atmosphere, 58, 59
Atomic explosions in sun, 9
Aurora borealis, 28
Autumn, 5, 328, 335
Avalanche, 275

Barite, 155
Barite crystal, 308
Bay, 241
Beach, 232, 238, 241, 252, 256
Bell buoy, 241
Beryl crystal, 309

Big Bear, constellation of, 25
Big Dipper, constellation of, 25, 221
Blizzard, 92
Borax, 49, 157
Borax crystal, 309
Breeze, 74, 76, 78, 241
Brook, 258, 260
Bryce Canyon, 314
Bull's eye, 155
Buoy, 241
Buried treasure game, 227

Canyon, 140, 173, 196
Caspian Sea, 177
Cave, 128, 136, 241, 313
Center of earth, 131
Chalk, 199
Channel, river, 196, 197, 263, 318
Cinnabar crystal, 309
City map, 215
Clay, 169, 199
Cliff, 140, 141, 173, 193, 199, 268
Cloud, 5, 12–15, 49, 61
  color of, 332, 333
  outer space, 106
  seeding of, 43
  shape of, 12, 13, 53
Coal, 33, 152
Collision of planets, 125

Comet, 103
Compass, 208, 221, 223, 225, 227
Condensation, 52, 53, 61, 67
Constellation, 25, 221
Corundum crystal, 309
Cosmic dust, 64, 65
Creek, 258, 260
Crystal, 49, 68, 308–311
Current
  air, 22, 76, 78, 79, 280, 281
  ocean, 255, 256, 272
  river, 271

Day and night, 328, 331–333
Dead Sea, 177
Desert, 85, 182, 185, 186, 188, 189, 190, 249
Devil's Tower, 314
Dew, 52, 53, 57, 66, 67
Diamond, 162, 163
Direction finding, 208, 209, 220–227
Downpour, 39
Drizzle, 38
Dry ice, 43
Dune, sand, 186
Dust, 39, 41, 49, 56, 57, 58, 63, 94
Dust cloud, 94
Dust devil, 85

Dust explosion, 283, 301
Dust in outer space, 64, 65, 106, 112, 118
Dust storm, 94
Dwarf star, 101

Earth, 112, 122, 126
  center of, 131
  heat of, 132, 244, 290, 293
  orbit of, 112
  position and seasons of, 334–336
  revolution of, 126
  rotation of, 126, 272, 331, 333
  satellite of, 338
  shape of, 307
  size of, 131
Earthquake, 132, 194, 195
  undersea, 252
Eclipse, 341, 343
Eddy, 271
Electricity
  northern light, 28
  outer space, 120, 121
  Saint Elmo's fire, 73
  water power, 269
Electric spark, 289, 301
Electric storm, 73, 120, 121, 288, 289
El Morro, 315
Emerald, 159
Energy from sunlight 33

Erosion
  water, 63, 165, 167, 185, 193, 196, 197, 268, 269, 276, 313–315
  wind, 63, 165, 167, 170, 171, 182, 193, 314, 315
Eruption, volcano, 290
Evaporation, 15, 36
Explosion
  atomic, in sun, 9
  dust, 301
  geyser, 294, 295
  natural, 282, 283
  tornado, 297
  underground, 290
  water formation, 298
Eye of hurricane, 89, 90

Falling star, 27
Finding direction, 208, 209, 220–227
Fire, 283, 285, 286, 287, 302
Fissure, 194, 195
Floating object, 236, 237
Flood, 264
  flash, 188, 189
Fog, 12, 56, 57, 61
Food from sunlight, 33
Fool's gold, 150
Forecasting weather, 13, 52–55
Forest, 173, 204
Forest fire, causes of, 283, 286, 287
Forms of water, 317
Frost, 56, 57, 68
Funnel, tornado and waterspout, 87

Galaxy, 122, 126
Gale, 79
Game
  Buried-treasure, 227
  Road-map, 218, 219
  What-is-it?, 326
Garlic stone, 157
Garnet crystal, 309
Gaseous state, 317
Gases
  air, 58, 59, 71
  comet, 103
  outer space, 106
  smoke, 61, 285
  sun, 9
Gemstones, 129, 158, 159, 162, 163
Geyser, 282, 294, 295
Glacier, 200, 251
Globe, 229
Gneiss, 148
Gold, 129, 147, 150
Gold crystal, 308
Gorge, 173, 196
  undersea, 140
Grand Canyon, 196
Granite, 148
Gravity, 111, 118
Great Salt Lake, 177
Gully, 193
Gypsum crystal, 309

Hail, 35, 47, 323
Halley's comet, 103
Heat
  earth, 144, 290
  sun, 9
Hematite, 155
High-pressure area, 82, 83
Hot spring, 179
Hurricane, 89, 90
Hurricane hunter, 90
Hydrogen in water, 298

Ice, 317
  erosion by, 276
  polar, 142, 143
Iceberg, 231, 251
Ice crystal, 49
Ice pellet, 323
Ice prism, 323
Icicle, 305, 321
Igneous rock, 148
Iron pyrite, 150
Island, 141
  formation of, 244

Jet stream, 280, 281
Jupiter, 112, 117

Lake, 173, 177, 229
  formation of, 175, 318
  oxbow, 318
Landslide, 276
Lava, 279, 293
Leo, constellation of, 25
Life on Mars, 112, 115
Light, 6, 9, 324
Lighthouse, 230, 247
Lightning, 73, 282, 288, 289
Light refraction, 11, 17, 18, 22
Limestone, 139
Liquid state, 317
Little Bear, constellation of, 25
Little Dipper, constellation of, 25
Loess, 170, 171
Low-pressure area, 83

Mackerel sky, 52, 53
Maelstrom, 271
Magnet, 65
  use in making compass, 223
Malachite, 155
Man in the moon, 20
Man-made satellite, 118
Maps, 208–229
Marble, 148
Mars, 112, 115, 117
Measuring rainfall, 45
Mercury, 112, 117
Metamorphic rock, 148
Meteor, 27, 64, 65
Meteorite, 27
Mica, 155
Milky Way, 122, 126
Mineral spring, 179

Mirage, 190
Moisture in air, 58, 59
Molten rock, 244, 279, 293
Monsoon, 93
Moods of sea, 256
Moon, 4, 122, 329
  eclipse of, 341, 343
  effect on tide of, 347
  man-made, 118
  mountains on, 20
  ring around, 18
  shadows on, 20
  shape of, 329, 338
  travel on, 108, 109
  travel to, 96, 118
Moon dogs, 18
Moons of other planets, 117
Mountain, 166, 167, 173, 229, 249, 275, 276, 307
  air mass, 82, 83
  formation of, 132, 290
  moon, 20
  under ocean, 129, 140, 141, 232, 244
Mud, 152, 199, 203

Natural bridge, 197
Nebula, 107, 122
Needles, The, South Dakota, 315
Neptune, 113, 117
Night and day, 328, 331–333
Northern lights, 28
North Pole, 28, 142, 143, 223, 251, 336
North Star, 221, 225

Oasis, 182
Ocean, 230–257, 272, 307, 344–347
Oil, 129, 144
Opal, 155
Orbit
  asteroid, 125
  comet, 103
  earth, 112, 126
Ore, metal, 150
Orion, constellation of, 25
Oxbow lake, 318
Oxygen in water, 298

Painted Desert, 185
Peat, 152
Pectolite, 155
Pegasus, constellation of, 25
Petrified Forest National Park, 161
Petrified wood, 161
Petroleum, See Oil
Pillars of sand, 85
Pilot, weather, 43
Pilot's chart, 229
Pirate map, 227
Plain, 175
Planet, 112, 113, 117, 125

Plants, 152, 203, 204
  energy stored in, 33, 152
Pluto, 113, 117
Points of compass, finding, 225
Precious stone, 128, 129, 158, 159, 162, 163
Pressure, air, 31, 90
Prism, 309
Profile Mountain, New Hampshire, 315
Pumice, 148
Purple mica, 155
Pyrite crystal, 309

Quartz crystal, 309
Quicksand, 207

Radio static, 121
Radio telescope, 105
Rain, 15, 17, 36–39, 42–45, 52–55, 63, 83, 89, 93, 135, 165, 171, 175, 179, 182, 188, 189, 260, 264
Rainbow, 17, 52, 53
Rain cloud, 13
Raindrop, 35, 47, 305, 323
Rainfall, measuring, 45
Rain forest, 173, 204
Rain gauge, 45
Rainmaking, 43
Rapids, 266
Red Sea, 177
Reef, 247
Refracted light, 11, 17, 18, 22
Revolution of earth, 126
Rhymes about weather, 52
Ring around moon, 18
Ring around sun, 18
Rings of Saturn, 112
River, 135, 175, 177, 193, 229, 258, 266
  cave formation by, 136
  changes in channel of, 132, 195, 196, 197, 263, 318
  desert, 188, 189
  flooding, 264
  source of, 260
  waterfall in, 268, 269
Riverbed, 266, 268
Road map, 209, 217
Road-map game, 218, 219
Rochelle salt, 311
Rock, 132, 146–167, 179, 180, 195, 199, 200, 241, 268, 269, 276, 290, 308, 309, 312–315
Rocket ship, 96, 97, 111, 125
Rotation of earth, 126, 331, 333
Ruby, 159

Sailor's chart, 229
Saint Elmo's fire, 73
Salt, 156, 305

Salt crystal, *49*, 308, 310
Salt Lake, 177
Sand, *49*, 148, 152, 165, 173, 182, 199, *207*, *238–241*, 248
Sand bar, 229, *242*, 247
Sand dune, 186
Sandstone, formation of, 148
Sandstorm, *94*
Sapphire, 159
Sargasso Sea, 231, *255*
Satellite, 117, 118, 338
Saturn, 112, 117
Sea, *See* Ocean
Sea level, 248, 249
Seasons, 328, 335, 336
Seaweed, 231, *241*, 255
Sedimentary rock, 148
Shadow, 20, 220, 324, *341* 343
Shape of earth, 307
Ship, dangers to, *242*, 247, 255
Shoal, 247
Shooting star, 27, *64*, 65
Silt, 318
Silver, 129
Silver crystal, 308
Silver iodide, rainmaking, *42*
Sky, *4, 5, 11, 12, 13*, 22, 25, 27, 28, 89, 235, 328, 332, 333
Skyline, 307
Slate, 148
Sleet, *47*, 323
Smog, 61
Smoke, *56, 57*, 61, *71*
Smokey Bear, *287*

Snow, 15, *41*, 50, 51, 83, *92*, 179, 180, 200, 260, *264*, 275, 321
Snowball, *41*, *50, 51*
Snowflake, *35, 41, 49, 305*, 323
Snow pellet, 323
Sodium chlorate, 311
Soil, 146, *147*, 169–171
Solar system, 112, 113
Solid state, 317
Soot in air, 63
Sound, speed of, 289
Source of river, 260
Southern lights, 28
South Pole, 28, 142, *143*, 251
Space storm, *120, 121*
Space travel, *96, 97*, 111, 118
Speed of lightning, 289
Speed of sound, 289
Spontaneous combustion, 302
Spring, season of, *5*, 328, 335
Spring, water, 179, 180
Sprinkle, *38*
Stalactite, *139*, 313
Stalagmite, *139*
Stars, *4, 9*, 22–25, 99, 101, 106, 122, 208, *209*, 221, 225
  shooting, 27, *64*, 65
  sound from, 105
States of matter, 317
Static, radio and telephone, 121
Staurolite crystal, 309
Steam, 244, 258, 295, 317

Stone Mountain, 314
Storm, 73, 89, 171, 247
  space, *120, 121*
Storm sign, 18
Stream, 258, 260
Sulfur, 157
Sulfur crystal, 308
Summer, *5*, 328, 333, 336
Sun, *4, 9*, 33, 36, 53, *96*, *118, 122, 125, 126*, 208, 209, 331, 332, 333, 338, 339, *341*, 343
Sunbeam, *6*
Sun dogs, 18
Sunlight, *6, 9, 11, 17*, 33
Sunrise, 328, 332, 333
Sunset, 328, 332, 333
Surf, *233, 238*, 252
Swamp, 173, 175, 203

Telescope, *99*, 112, 113, 122
Thunder, 289
Tidal wave, 252
Tide, 329, 346, 347
Topaz, 159
Topaz crystal, 308
Tornado, *85, 87*, 297
Tunnel in cave, 136
Turquoise, 159
Turquoise crystal, 309

Underground rock, 129, 132, 135, 179, 199
Underground water, 129, 135, 136, 179, 180, 294
Undersea mountain, 129, 140, 141, 232, 244
Unusual stars, 101

Uranus, 113, 117

Venus, 112
Volcano, *141*, 148, 185, *244*, 279, 282, 293, 298

Water, 135, 139, 179, 180, 203, 232, 233, 235–237, 241, 242, 244, 247, 248, 249, 256, 270, 271, 272, 294, 295, 298, 317, 321
Water crystal, *49*
Water erosion, 63, 165, 167, 185, 193, 196, 197, *268, 269*, 276, 313, 314, 315
Waterfall, *17*, 268, 269
Waterspout, *87*
Waves, *232, 237*, 242, 252, 256, 329, 344, 345
Weather, 12–19, 34–61, 66–69, 73, 82, 83, 89–94
  See also Storm; Wind
Weather forecasting, 52–55
Weatherstone, 155
Weightlessness, 111
Well, 135, 180
What-is-it?, game, 326
Whirlpool, 270, 271
Whitecap, *232*, 256
Wind, 15, *47*, 74–95, 182, 186, 230, 238, 280, 281, 297
Wind erosion, 63, 165, 167, 170, 171, 182, 193, 314, 315
Winter, *5*, 328, 335, 336
Wood, burning, *71*